I0461226

Spiritual Nurturing for Intuitive Children

Training Parents to Embrace and Enhance Their Psychic Child's Abilities

MICHELLE HENDERSON

Copyright © 2022 by Michelle Henderson.

All rights reserved. No part of this publication may be reproduced, distributed, or transmitted in any form or by any means, including photocopying, recording, digital scanning, or other electronic or mechanical methods, without the prior written permission of the publisher, except in the case of brief quotations embodied in critical reviews and certain other noncommercial uses permitted by copyright law. For permission requests, write to the author at the email below.

ISBN Paperback: 979-8-9853253-1-7

Library of Congress Control Number: 2021924257

Printed in the United States of America.

Michelle Henderson
info@MichelleHendersonMedium.com

Although this publication is designed to provide accurate information in regard to the subject matter covered, the publisher and the author assume no responsibility for errors, inaccuracies, omissions, or any other inconsistencies herein. This publication is meant as a source of valuable information for the reader, however, it is not meant as a replacement for direct expert assistance. If such a level of assistance is required, the services of a competent professional should be sought.

Illustrations List / List of Photos

I dedicate this book to our intuitive children who experience metaphysical events and to those who teach these children how to embrace their spiritual gifts. Our world needs our children to teach what true love and acceptance really is.

I also want to dedicate the book to my father, Harry Odum, for modeling what being an author truly is. His love of reading books gave him the inspiration to write his own stories. I know that his spirit is with me as I write each word. He always told me he had spiritual help!

Acknowledgments

When people build a house, they have to contact different individuals with various talents, expertise, and knowledge to make their dream a reality. First, construction workers complete the foundation of the house, then they build the walls, windows, and roof. Finally, they complete the interior of the house, and the people move in and make the house a home.

Creating this book has been a bit like building a house. God gave me the personality, talent, experience, and passion to work with children throughout my life. When creating this book, the Divine gave me the ideas, inspiration, and guidance needed to spread knowledge that will help our children fulfill their spiritual journeys.

While completing research for this book, all the talents that spiritual people shared amaze me. I want to thank Giselle Shardlow, founder of the online platform Kids Yoga Stories, for allowing me to include the chakra yoga poses and breathing techniques she uses while teaching children.

This book would not be as inspiring without the childhood stories of psychic mediums: Peri Zarrella, Ryan Michaels, Allison DuBois, Lisa Williams, and Tamara Hermann. Thank you all for sharing your stories with the world, for creating a pathway for our intuitive children to follow, and for creating a supportive space in which they can embrace their spiritual gifts.

My editor, Michael Ireland, gave the book life. I could see the words I wrote morphed into poetry. Thank you, Michael, for sharing your God-given talent with me.

The self-publishing consulting firm, PRESStinely, LLC, inspired me and their guidance led to this fabulous product. Thanks to the whole PRESStinely team for their vision.

This book would not have been possible without the love and support of my husband and family. They have always believed in all my creative ideas and have given me the faith I needed during the times I questioned my spirituality.

From my heart, thank you all.

Table of Contents

Introduction – Why Parent Training?

If you are a psychic, medium, or spiritual coach, and you have been wanting to work with families and their children, this book is for you. I have worked with children for over thirty years, and I continue to be amazed at what children can teach us. The saying, "Look at the world through a child's eyes" has been a precious one for me.

Children come into this world with a fresh perspective—they are as spiritual as anyone can be. Just as a seed planted in rich soil will grow into a beautiful flower, a child will grow strong in an environment that has the essentials they need to survive (such as food, water, shelter, and air). But with just the essentials, will a child's spiritual growth increase as well? I believe children need physical *and* spiritual nurturing, and this book is about providing spiritual nourishment to children.

Parents, society, and communities can influence a child's spiritual growth, and I believe that everyone who walks a spiritual path from an early age will find their true purpose in life. This has been true for me and my family. I grew up in Abilene, Texas, which is in the "bible belt" of the United States. Every Sunday, my family and I would attend services at our community church, and I'd go to Sunday school. I embraced the love, forgiveness, faith, and non-judgmental teachings of Jesus, and have always been grateful for my religious upbringing. My relationship with Jesus extends outside the bounds of the religious sector, and on my spiritual journey over a lifetime, I have strengthened my spiritual, intuitive relationship with Jesus.

As far back as I can remember, I have always followed my intuition. But as I grew up, my intuition became stronger—I felt different energies, felt spirit's presence, and heard spirit voices. It wasn't long before I started talking to spirits. When I shared my loving spiritual experiences with family and friends, I was told: "Don't open that door!" Everyone told me not to pursue the spiritual realm—they were afraid of what might happen.

So, it wasn't until years later that I embraced my authentic self. I learned that other psychics and mediums had similar experiences when they were younger. For example, if they communicated with a relative who had passed, they were told, "Stop it!" If they saw apparitions, their parents told them, "That's evil, stop." So, they shunned their intuitive abilities, and forgot them—until later in life. What if, instead of discouraging their children's spiritual growth, these parents had been educated about the spiritual world? They could have nourished it instead! If only they had known.

Knowledge gives people power and control of their lives. I am a behavioral analyst, and as a part of my child-client's behavioral treatment plan, one of my job responsibilities was to complete Parent Training. Training parents to implement behavioral strategies was an integral part of improving their child's behavior—even after the clinical professionals were no longer part of the child's life. Those parents gained knowledge to help them embrace and nurture their child's abilities and growth.

This is why I wrote this book. Just as behavioral strategies helped those parents to help their children on a physical level, parents need processes, procedures, and plans so they can help their children on the spiritual level, too. Whether you are a licensed child therapist, a psychologist, a professional lightworker, or an adult seeking ways to help a child, this book is for you. I hope the information I have presented will inspire your passion, offer insight, and assist you in educating parents about elements of spirituality that will help every child fulfill his or her spiritual journey in all phases of their lives.

1
Intuitive Abilities and Spirituality

Children with Intuitive Abilities

"Nanna told me to tell you hello." What a wonderful thing for a child to say to a parent. Unless, of course, Nanna has been deceased for years—then that statement can frighten, even terrify, its recipient. Yet greetings from the spirit world such as this one are common among children with psychic and mediumship abilities.

So, how do you know if a child is a psychic, a medium—or both? Here are some behaviors a child may exhibit that can be signs that he or she has intuitive abilities:

1. The child knows and understands the feelings of others in different situations (they are empathic).
2. They have an imaginary friend. Many theories suggest a child's imaginary friend might be their spirit guide.
3. They perceive energies in different environments. For example, a child may become sad in one environment, and excited in a different environment. Many children who feel these kinds of energy may be fearful of crowded places.
4. They see and talk to family members who have passed on.
5. They may report having an out-of-body experience or a dream in which they felt they were flying or were in a different reality. Children who have these types of dreams may experience sleepless nights.

6. They remember a past life or talk about memories from another time and place, or they may share names of people from their past or talk about experiences they have had with a different family.
7. They may have a close bond with an animal.
8. They may gaze above someone's head, and if this is a common practice, they may be looking at another person's aura (a colorful field of (usually) invisible energy around a person's body).
9. They may be very creative.

In her book *Your Psychic Child*, author and teacher Sara Wiseman discusses age-level behaviors of children with intuitive abilities.[1] According to Wiseman, between the ages of three and five, most children become curious about everything, but intuitive children also become afraid of the dark and tell their parents they fear the monsters in their bedroom. Often, these children have visions of the past, present, and future, and exhibit some or all of the behaviors outlined on the list above.

Between the ages of six to eight, most children become independent thinkers. They are old enough to consider future decisions and to become mindful of following society's rules. It is during this stage that parents should teach their children how to strengthen their intuitive abilities. They can teach children different strategies to nurture their spiritual selves:

➤ meditation,
➤ breathing exercises,
➤ yoga,
➤ how to connect with the Divine, and
➤ how to communicate with their spirit team.

Between the ages of nine and twelve, many children feel peer pressure and want their peers to accept them. So, they may decide to hide their intuitive abilities from their peers. Their loved ones may witness them becoming more isolated from the family and becoming self-reliant. Since by this age children can concentrate for longer periods, they can take part in longer yoga classes, meditation sessions, and other spiritual practices, and become more accepting of their intuitive skills.

Between the ages of thirteen and fifteen, puberty begins, and children experience changes emotionally, physically, mentally, and socially. Intuitive children may question what spirituality means to them, and may consider different religions and traditions. Their intuitive abilities might be as strong as an adult's—and they may even heal others.

At sixteen, children become even more autonomous. As they strive to discover their identity, they may experiment with dark cults, alcohol, or drugs. At this age, any child who is strengthening their intuitive abilities will benefit from the services of a professional psychic medium. A psychic medium who completes a reading with a minor (anyone under eighteen years of age) will need to get permission from the child's parents or request the parents be present during the reading. Any practitioner under eighteen who completes a reading with a another person under eighteen will need to obtain permission from both the practitioner's parents and the sitter's parents.

---

[1] Wiseman, Sara. *Your Psychic Child: How to Raise Intuitive and Spiritually Gifted Kids of All Ages*. St. Paul, MN: Llewellyn, 2011. Kindle.

Because these children lack life experience and emotional maturity, it will be difficult for them to do psychic or mediumship readings for others.

Indigo Children

In the late 1960s, parapsychologist Nancy Ann Tappe coined the term "Indigo Child." She developed a system that analyzed a person's personality based upon the hue of his or her aura. Nancy considered herself a synesthete, someone who perceives sensory stimulus in an atypical manner. For example, synesthetes may hear color or see sound. Nancy could see auras around people, and noticed that many children she interfaced with had the color indigo dominant in their auras. So, she named them "Indigo Children." According to the blogger named "blom.10," Nancy believes that Indigo children are "spiritually evolved souls reincarnating on Earth born with the purpose of starting a spiritual evolution for all humans."[2] Many experts have concluded that, besides having similar auras, Indigo children have other parallel characteristics, including:

> They are born with spiritual gifts; they are aware of the spiritual world; and they may say that their goals are to help others become more spiritual.
> They expect others to live as they do—with honesty, respect, and pride. They expect others to be responsible, to generate trust, and to help others.
> They do not understand why others have different philosophies and observe different religious doctrines.
> Their strong intuition has led them to hold different ideas and beliefs about the world.
> They live their lives feeling that the world is a false reality, and they eschew authority.
> They become leaders, develop warrior personalities, and oppose how world societies have advanced.
> They feel they are lost souls, and may isolate themselves from others.
> They are unwilling to change themselves to fit in.
> They can experience low self-esteem and as they go through the adolescent years, they feel they don't fit in.
> They may self-medicate with drugs and alcohol as they try to cope with world issues.
> They may face depression and may be diagnosed with ADHD (Attention-Deficit / Hyperactivity Disorder), because they view life with intense feelings and emotions.

American writer and public personality Doreen Virtue stated in her book, *The Care and Feeding of Indigo Children*, that she sees a "correlation between attention deficit issues and being spiritually evolved." In her opinion, ADHD stands for "Attention Dials to Higher Dimensions."[3]

Autism Spectrum Disorders

If you, as a therapist, choose to work with children with intuitive abilities, you may encounter children who have been diagnosed with an autism spectrum disorder (ASD). For example, well-

---

[2] blom.10, "Are You an Indigo Child Too?," *The Psychology of Extraordinary Beliefs*, April 16, 2019, https://u. osu.edu/vanzandt/2019/04/16/indigo-child-movement/.

[3] Virtue, Doreen. *The Care and Feeding of Indigo Children*. Alexandra, N.S.W.: Hay House, 2006, Kindle.

known psychic medium William Stillman, the author of a trilogy that explores the spiritual gifts autistics display, was diagnosed with Asperger's Syndrome under DSM-IV criteria.[4] According to the autism advocacy group, Autism Speaks, "In 2020, the Centers for Disease Control and Prevention reported that approximately 1 in 54 children will be diagnosed with an autism spectrum disorder."[5] William Stillman's opinion of why so many children are being diagnosed with autism is that:

> ...[The] reflection of our recent history is that the world requires more love, compassion, and tolerance amidst ever-mounting global concerns. This is our Creator's purposeful plan to refocus us on the importance of reverence for all humanity. After all, so many individuals with autism are all about love.[6]

Stillman believes that children with autism who do not communicate with others and who sit motionless might communicate telepathically. He compares this form of communication with meditation and prayer. These children experience and embrace spiritual events without judgment, and, because of a deficit in their social awareness, they may believe that everyone encounters spiritual events. If you are working with a child with autism who is communicating through telepathy instead of verbally, you can create a social story with pictures that explain what he or she is doing.

I can talk to others by using my mind.	Some people cannot hear me.
I will need to use my voice or my communication device.	Everyone communicates differently.

---

[4] Stillman, William. *Autism and the God Connection: Redefining the Autistic Experience through Extraordinary Accounts of Spiritual Giftedness*. Naperville, IL: Sourcebooks, Inc., 2006. Kindle.
[5] "Autism Statistics and Facts," Autism Speaks, accessed September 26, 2021, https://www.autismspeaks.org/autism-statistics-asd.
[6] Stillman, 2006

Writer and autism advocate Lisa Jo Rudy interviewed William Stillman about his work as an autism consultant. He stated that children with autism can connect to the Divine and have spiritual experiences. These children, Stillman says, are adept at:

> ...animal communication, communion with a loved one in Spirit, [and they] have information ... about their previous lives, [they see] apparitions of wayward souls ("ghosts"), and [they can commune] with benign, ethereal entities, defined as angels by some. I came to understand that, for those predisposed, these experiences were very common—natural, not supernatural. [7]

Loved ones who have crossed over surround each of us; we all have spirit guides and angels to assist us on our journey through life. It is not unusual, therefore, for a special-needs child to feel or see their own spirit team and to have spiritual experiences. Remember that when you are dealing with spiritual events, you are working with the soul of a child; you are not treating their physical disability. When you are working with a child with intuitive abilities and their family, in order to create a Family Service plan, it is important to know the child's background and diagnosis.

Spirituality

Everyone is born understanding and knowing the different dimensions of spirituality. But what is spirituality? Pediatrician Dr. Mya Spencer puts it best: "Spirituality involves the recognition of a feeling or sense or belief that there is something greater than myself, something more to being human than sensory experience, and that the greater whole of which we are part is cosmic or divine in nature."[8] Other scholars agree. For example, as American writer and researcher Louis Delgran tells us in her online article, *What is Spirituality*, "People may describe a spiritual experience as sacred or transcendent or simply a deep sense of aliveness and interconnectedness."[9]

Exploring what spirituality means to us may take a lifetime. Someone who experiences a miracle, for example, may develop a different meaning of what spirituality is compared to someone who experiences a tragedy. A professor of Psychology and Education at Columbus University, Lisa Miller, has done extensive research into the link between scientific knowledge and the power of spirituality and how spirituality can affect the health and life of a child. As Miller says in her book *The Spiritual Child*, science has concluded that "...spirituality is inborn, fundamental to the human constitution, [and] central in our physiology and psychology. Spirituality links brain, mind and body."[10] Based on this assessment, we see it is vital that children with intuitive abilities continue to grow spiritually. If children develop an interconnected relationship with God and they experience

---

[7] Lisa Jo Rudy, "Autism and Spirituality," Verywell Health, accessed April 18, 2021, https://www.verywellhealth.com/autism-and-spirituality-260300.

[8] Maya Spencer, "What Is Spirituality? A Personal Exploration," Royal College of Psychiatrists, 2012, https://www.rcpsych.ac.uk/docs/default-source/members/sigs/spirituality-spsig/what-is-spirituality-maya-spencer-x.pdf?sfvrsn=f28df052_2.

[9] Lois Delgran, "What Is Spirituality?," Taking Charge of Your Health & Wellbeing, Accessed September 26, 2021, https://www.takingcharge.csh.umn.edu/what-spirituality.

[10] Miller, Lisa. *The Spiritual Child: The New Science on Parenting for Health and Lifelong Thriving*, 25. New York: Picador/St. Martin's Press, 2016. Kindle.

trauma or difficulties in their lives, they will turn to God for guidance. This spiritual relationship will deter them from turning to drugs or alcohol to stop the pain they may be feeling. Spirituality is an anchor in these children's lives. But remember, religion and spirituality are not the same thing. Mainstream religion will only help these children if they are working with internal faith and are connected with the spiritual realm through having a personal, transcendent relationship with the Divine.

As children learn and grow through childhood developmental levels in the cognitive, social, emotional, and physical areas of their lives, their spirituality integrates into these areas. Dr. Lisa Miller and her colleges completed a longitudinal research study to determine if adults who displayed strong religious or spiritual beliefs had thicker cortices in their brain than adults who did not have religious or spiritual beliefs and how belief systems affect a family's health. With the use of brain imaging technology, the research concluded that if people live a spiritual lifestyle, their cerebral cortex will benefit in positive ways and they will be able to deal with life crises. If someone is depressed, however, the region of the cortex will not be as healthy, and will appear thinner. Thus, to have a healthy adult brain, one must start with a healthy brain in childhood.

Brain damage (or impairment) in a child's early years can result from physical, mental, or emotional triggers. For example, if a child experiences trauma, a stress hormone (cortisol) will increase and can not only damage the brain but will slow that child's growth. Such an outcome is preventable (and alterable) if a traumatized child grows up in a home that embraces spirituality. With parental moral support and encouragement, a traumatized child's spiritual growth will flourish.

Most parents develop dreams for their children when they are born—they want them to become productive, independent, and successful adults. But as everyday life unfolds and challenging events arise, sometimes the best-laid plans go awry. For many parents, building a spiritual foundation can ease some trials and tribulations of life and help their children grow up feeling supported and empowered—physically, mentally, emotionally, and spiritually.

But how do parents teach their children to become spiritual? It is not unusual, for example, for two parents to have different religious beliefs, and this can confuse their children. How should parents of different faiths teach their children to be spiritual? Should they join a church, synagogue, or mosque? Should they find a metaphysical community or join a spiritual group? It's a tough decision (and one every parent must face in their child's life). And, of course, there is always the option of not teaching spirituality at all.

Some parents may choose not to teach or support their child's spiritual growth because of the negative experiences they faced with their own spiritual growth. In such cases, by ignoring their child's questions and experiences, parents may hinder their child's spiritual awakening.

All children are born to develop their own spiritual pathway, and parents of intuitive children should consider their child's spiritual health—for intuitive children going through adolescence who do not have a strong personal relationship with the Divine may turn to darker energies or may even join a cult. So, for therapists working with children and their families, it is important to know and understand what the family's religious or spiritual beliefs are without judgment. Overall, spirituality is a human experience that can teach us we are connected to something greater than ourselves. Everyone has their unique encounters with the distinct elements of spirituality.

Exercise: Vision Board

The purpose of this exercise is for parents to create a vision board which illustrates spiritual goals they want their child to achieve in the next ten years. Parents will need a cork or poster board at least 22 x 18 inches, a glue stick, magazines, and a picture of their child.

To put the vision board together, parents should place their child's picture in the middle of the board. Each parent should sit and set an intention, such as "What do I want my child's spiritual life to look like?" Then, parents should find pictures in magazines that represent goals that fulfill their stated intention. When finished, the vision board should be filled with uplifting images that both inspire and empower the family. The family should hang the board in their home where they can see it daily. Older children can create their own spiritual visual board with or without their parents.

2

Intake – Embracing the Whole Child

Many families in spiritual crisis may not know where to turn when they need help. When the spiritual crisis involves a psychic or mediumistic child, the crisis is amplified. These parents are afraid that if they go to a medical doctor seeking support, the physician might medicate their child. If they go to a counselor or to a psychiatrist looking for answers, they may find themselves in a financial crisis. If they go to their church, they may feel judged. If they go to a holistic healer, they may be afraid it will not work. This spiritual crisis may continue for years.

Such families need support from someone who can guide them and help them to connect with the spiritual world. When parents reach out, as a therapist or lightworker, you need to communicate constructively. If parents are going to consider your spiritual recommendations, you must earn their trust, and to do that, you must develop a strategy that will:

> ➤ engender confidence in your skills (your therapeutic, mediumistic, and other professional talents),
> ➤ provide parents with comprehensive information about the services you offer, and
> ➤ provide you with data you can use to develop a plan for your clients and their child.

So, before you provide a family service, I suggest you create an Intake Form containing a set of standard questions to ask all onboarding clients. You can have the parents complete the Intake Form themselves before their first appointment with you first appointment, or you can interview the parents and complete the questionnaire with them. The form should contain a written contract that provides a clear declaration of the services you offer. You may also wish to provide families with other resources (such as business cards of other professionals) that will benefit the family's healing process. Below, I have provided questions and information you should include in an Intake Form.

Questions and Information

On the top of the parent Intake Form, place your logo, your business name, and the nature of the service you are providing. To gain the parents' trust, ensure there is a declaration in a prominent place on the form that all information they provide about their child and their family will remain confidential. If you are working with a colleague or partner, let your clients know who else will have access to this information.

Michelle Henderson Medium
Spiritual Family Services
Intake Questionnaire

All information on this document is Confidential.

1. Child's Name: _____ 2. D.O.B. _____ 3. Age:_____

4. Your Name: _____ 5. Relationship to Child:_____

6. Describe in Detail why you want Spiritual Family Services.

7. How long has the child experienced these distressing issues/events?

When you are planning to create a spiritual training program for a family, here are some vital items you should add to your Intake Form:

- ➤ the child's age.
- ➤ the child's developmental level. You do not want to create a spiritual program for children if they are not "ready" or are not mature enough to complete a spiritual task.
- ➤ the child's diagnosis. (If a child has a medical or mental health history, you need to know how this affects the child's daily life, and how it is affecting the family unit.)
- ➤ the reasons the family is reaching out for spiritual help.
- ➤ the family's religious preference, if any.
- ➤ how long the family has been in crisis. (The longer the crisis, the more stressors are placed on each family member.)
- ➤ what spiritual stressors affect areas in the child's life (see chart below). (If stressors in any area are affecting the child severely, discover what other resources and services the family has used in the past. Through this information, you will know what resources and services worked or did not work for the child.)

If you do not feel qualified to help a family in a spiritual crisis, refer them to another professional. You have intuitive gifts and can help others, but if you don't have all the tools to help a family, be honest.

The chart below outlines the levels of spiritual stressors many families of psychic children experience. The second chart below reveals most of the behaviors exhibited by children who have intuitive abilities (or the results of having these abilities).

Spiritual Stressors

In Daily Life	Not at All	Minimally	Moderately	Significantly/Severely
Academically	Not at All	Minimally	Moderately	Significantly/Severely
Within the Family	Not at All	Minimally	Moderately	Significantly/Severely
Interpersonally/Socially	Not at All	Minimally	Moderately	Significantly/Severely

Circle the behaviors that you see your child do.

- anxious/worried
- anger, aggression, violence
- crying or tearful
- feel how others feel
- withdrawn/alone
- school issues
- hears voices
- see apparitions/ghosts
- knows what others think
- predict events
- feels different energies
- special bond with animals
- sleep problems
- fearful of a room
- meditates daily
- uses tools-Ouija board
- family member with intuitive abiliites

- fascination with metaphysical things
- fascinated with occult
- can see colors around others
- has many friends
- talks about dreams/nightmares
- talks about past life
- loves to spend time in nature
- sees spirits around others
- has an imaginary friend
- peers make fun of their abilities
- has a great imagination
- is creative
- sees relatives who has passed
- has strong empathy
- prays daily
- uses tools such as crystals, tarot cards, oracle cards

Religion and Spirituality

When you understand how your client family practices their religion, you can provide valuable spiritual and intuitive information the family will feel comfortable implementing. If your recommendations are not compatible with the family's beliefs, however, they will be ineffective. So, to determine whether a client family will accept your recommendations, ask questions about their religious and spiritual beliefs.

Religious Preferences

1. Is your family a member of an organized religion? If so, explain which one and what practices do you take part of?

2. Do you consider your family spiritual? Why?

3. What spiritual guidance or knowledge are you hoping for?

Medical and Mental Health History

Psychic children display many atypical sensory abilities that professionals not trained in the psychic sciences can miss. For example, many patients diagnosed with mental disorders defined in the *Diagnostic and Statistical Manual of Mental Disorders 5th Edition* (*DSM*-5) have deficits in sensory processing or have abnormalities in sensory sensitivity. As neuroscientist Laura A. Harrison et al. state in their article, "The Importance of Sensory Processing in Mental Health: A Proposed Addition to the Research Domain Criteria (RDoC) and Suggestions for RDoC 2.0," "Sensory sensitivity plays an important role in sensory processing sensitivity (SPS), a personality trait, as well as in the clinical symptomatology of sensory processing in ASD, sensory processing disorder (SPD), depression, and anxiety disorders."[11]

You will need to determine how to work with the child in your care and to base your strategies on a child's diagnosis. In some assessments of psychic and mediumistic children, psychologists, psychiatrists, and other medical professionals (who use the *DSM* as their definitive guide for

---

[11] Laura A. Harrison, et al. "The Importance of Sensory Processing in Mental Health: A Proposed Addition to the Research Domain Criteria (Rdoc) and Suggestions for Rdoc 2.0," *Frontiers in Psychology* 10 (2019), https://doi.org/10.3389/fpsyg.2019.00103.

psychological medicine) wrongly diagnose psychic children with amplified sensory abilities as having sensory deficit disorders. For example, they may identify children who hear voices or see things that "are not there" as having schizophrenia. Associate professors of psychiatry and psychologist at Yale, Philip Corlett and Albert Powers, and associate professor at the University of Nebraska, Megan S. Kelly, completed a study that compared clairaudient mediums with patients diagnosed with a psychotic disorder who hear voices daily, and patients diagnosed with a psychotic disorder who never hear voices. They reported that "We found the hallucinatory experiences of psychic voice-hearers to be very similar to those of patients who were diagnosed. We employed techniques from forensic psychiatry to conclude that the psychics were not malingering."[12]

All the mediums in the study stated that they believed the voices they heard came from a higher spiritual plane, from the Divine, or from a spiritual being present during the interview. The people diagnosed with a psychotic disorder said that hearing voices was distressing, and that they felt there was something wrong with their brain.

When children have intuitive abilities, they are using so-called "Clair Senses" (see definitions below) that correspond with the five physical senses: seeing, hearing, feeling, smelling, and tasting. The ability to tap into the clair senses is a natural talent, but everyone develops this gift at different stages in their lives—and some never develop it at all. But for children who are learning about their spiritual abilities, it's difficult to navigate the current medical system to discover what is "wrong with them." Most times, nothing is wrong with them at all, and they have found their way to you.

Medical Information

1. Please list any medical (diabetes, cancer, hearing or vision problems, sensory integration disorder, etc.) that your child has been diagnosed.

2. Please list any mental health history (such as ADHD, Autism, Anxiety, Learning Disabilities, Bipolar Disorder, Schizophrenia, etc.) your child has been diagnosed.

---

[12] Albert R. Powers, et al. "Varieties of Voice-Hearing: Psychics and the Psychosis Continuum." *Schizophrenia Bulletin* 43, no. 1 (2016): 84–98, https://doi.org/10.1093/schbul/sbw133.

Physical Elements

Empathic children may develop sensory overload because of their heightened senses. For example, sounds may be louder, colors maybe brighter, and the taste of foods might be more intense.

Please inital the statement below.

Do you understand that the Spiritual Family Services that Michelle Henderson LLC offers are considered a holistic service, not a medical service?

A holistic approach is a service that views the whole person, not just their mental health needs. It supports a person's physical, emotional, social and spiritual wellbeing.

_____Yes   _____No

They may develop more stomachaches, heart palpitations, episodes of breathlessness, or headaches.

*

As noted earlier, if a psychic child develops physical or mental symptoms after experiencing a stressful situation (or sensory overload), their parents may take them to a medical doctor or to a psychologist for help. When a psychic child sees a medical professional, they may learn that their reactions are "not normal" and that there is "something wrong with them." Thereafter, it would not be unusual for a child who uses his or her clair senses to develop a fear of the energy or the spiritual event he or she is experiencing.

Legal Disclosure

As noted above, parents need to understand the type of services you are offering, and that you are not offering registered therapeutic counseling or medical services. If you work as a psychic medium, spiritual healer, or lightworker, you need to clarify your role and service to the parents, and the parents must acknowledge their understanding by signing an appropriate form. See below.

Please inital the statement below.

Do you understand that **Michelle Henderson** will provide spiritual services as a psychic medium? This will NOT include services such as medical, counseling, behavior, or psychiatric services? Resources will be provided to assist in your child's and family's needs during services.

_____Yes   _____No

Many parents of psychic children will seek services that are cheaper than counseling or medical treatment. They may seek an alternative therapy because they have had a negative experience with a counselor or a medical practitioner. If the parents know you are working as a psychic medium, they must realize that you are not a therapist, counselor, or doctor. Again, you need to clarify how you will implement your spiritual services.

Please inital the statement below.

Do you understand that all information is offered for personal and entertainment purposes and is not intended at any time to replace the advice, counsel or recommendations of any medical, psychological, legal or financial expert or any other professional services? Mediumship and Psychic work is experimental in nature and information imparted during a session is open to interpretation. Clients are advised that they have free will at all times to make their own choices and **Michelle Henderson** shall not be held responsible for the actions they may or may not take as a result of the session.

_____Yes _____No

To protect yourself and your business, such a waiver is important, so both parties agree how and in what capacity you will provide your services.

Please sign below.

I have completed the form with information that is accurate to my knowledge and I give Michelle Henderson, LLC permission to give my child and my family Spirituality Family Services.

_____
Signature

Financial Issues

During the Intake process, you will also want to establish the financial aspects of the services, and when payment will be due.

Finances

1. Michelle Henderson LLC accepts all major credit cards through Paypal.
2. Payments will be due on the first day of every month. A late fee of $20.00 will incur if the payment is 5 days late.
3. If the family wants to cancel services, a written statement should be sent to Michelle Henderson LLC two weeks before payment is due.

Acquiring Comprehensive Information

While completing the Intake Process, it can be difficult to obtain all the useful information you need to create an effective Family Service Plan. One way to encourage the family to give additional information about their child's spiritual and paranormal experiences is to create a video segment. Below is an exercise that will not only motivate the family to provide additional information but also inspire each family member to provide their perspectives and opinions about these experiences.

Exercise: Creating a News Segment

Because of advances in technology, it is easy for people to create video clips. Many children love to be the star of the show. This exercise is a fun, creative way to get additional information from families you will work with. Parents can use the video feature on a phone, computer, or a video camera.

First, parents should develop questions they can ask their child about the spiritual events he or she has been experiencing and then write a script they can follow to create an imaginary news segment. An innovative opening to the video segment could be, "Welcome to the Henderson's news. Today I am interviewing Sally."

Older children can create their own news segment by taking on the role of news anchor and explaining their spiritual events.

Have fun and be creative!

3

Developing a Family Training Program

Knowledge Is Powerful

With the information you gathered during the Intake, you are ready to create a spiritual program to not only help a child with their situation but also to help educate their parents. Remember, parents may tell you that you don't need the information you are requesting they provide—but believe me, you do!

When families are in crisis, they may not make rational decisions. The method in which you deliver the information will reinforce trust, strengthen the relationship between you and the parents, and assuage any fears the family may have. So, as much as you can, involve the parents in your work with their child. As physicist Marie Curie once said, "Nothing in life is to be feared, it is only to be understood." [13] So true! Education and information provide power. Remember:

> ➤ When a client family completes their work with you, they will have to use the tools and resources you have given them.
> ➤ The more quality information you can provide, the less a family will rely on you in order to feel safe.
> ➤ Every situation will be unique. What works with one family will not work for another.

Referrals

If you cannot create an effective Family Training Program for a client, it is time to refer them to someone else. Keep a list of therapists, medical professional, counselors, and lightworkers on file so you can refer your clients to a trusted colleague. Having business cards of professionals you know and trust on hand to share with families can be extremely helpful.

---

[13] https://www.brainyquote.com/quotes/marie_curie_389010

Creating a Program

On the following page, I have provided information and exercises you can incorporate into your practice and use when starting your program. When customizing which elements to use for each family, take the child's developmental age into account. Parents will tell you if they don't think their child is ready for certain information or specific exercises. The parents can always use the information you give them at a later time.

Terminology

1. Empath:

According to freelance journalist Victoria Stokes, "Intuitive empaths are believed to be a unique kind of empath that combines empathy, or the ability to understand and share the feelings of others, with instinct and perception."[14]

Many children may be overwhelmed by knowing how others are feeling and may not understand that these feelings are not their own. According to Judith Orloff, MD, author of *The Empath's Survival Guide: Life Strategies for Sensitive People*, there are six types of empaths: the "physical empath, the emotional empath, the intuitive empath, the plant empath, the Earth empath, and the animal empath." [15]

2. Mediumship:

Evidential Medium Debbie Wojciechowski explains mediumship in a succinct way: "In the world of spiritualism, 'medium' refers to a person with psychic ability [who is able] to produce phenomena of a physical or mental nature by communicating with spirit. Mediums can listen to and relay messages from 'the other side,' as well as communicate with loved ones who have crossed over."[16] When it comes to the families you are working with, it is helpful for parents to know that children are natural mediums, and that often, the spirits they are communicating with are family members who have passed on to the spirit world. Knowing this can be comforting to a family who feels distraught about what is happening to their child.

3. Psychic:

A psychic forms an energetic connection with another person to read information contained within the person's aura (called a "soul-to-soul connection"). They use their intuition to receive information about someone's past, present, or future (or all three). Many psychics will use tools such as Oracle decks or Tarot cards during psychic readings to assist them in tapping into the energy field of their sitter and interpreting in words the information they receive energetically.

Psychic children are born with the innate ability to connect into other people's auras. These children use different "psychic clairs" (see below) during a psychic experience.

---

[14] Victoria Stokes, "Intuitive Empaths: Signs, Types, Downsides, and Self-Care," Healthline Media, April 6, 2021, https://www.healthline.com/health/intuitive-empaths.

[15] Judith Orloff. *The Empath's Survival Guide: Life Strategies for Sensitive People*. Boulder, CO: Sounds True, Inc., 2018.

[16] Debbie Wojciechowski, "What Is a Medium?," Debbie Wojciechowski - Evidential Medium, November 11, 2019, https://mediumdebbie.com/blog/2019/10/30/what-is-a-medium.

4. The Clairs:
There are eight clairs psychic children might use during an intuitive episode.

➤ Claircognizance (sense of knowing)
"'Claircognizance' or 'clear knowing' is the pathway of extra-sensory perception (ESP) that manifests as spontaneous factual knowledge and information. It also produces baffling insights, deep inherent wisdom, and even inspired ideas and solutions to complex problems."[17] People who use claircognizance will know about ideas and incidents before they happen. The Divine, spirit guides, or their higher self may give them this information to guide them to make rational decisions through their lives, to help others, and to increase their spiritual knowledge.

➤ Clairsentience (clear sensation or feeling)
Clairsentience is the perception of information via a feeling within the whole body, despite receiving no outer stimuli or information related to the feeling. Psychic children use clairsentience daily to navigate through life; they can feel which adults are safe to be around, and they "think with their heart."

As we get older, we stop thinking with our heart and ignore the information we get from our clairsentience. As writer Liane Mandalis says in her article, "Clairsentience," "We are then taught to only trust what we see with our eyes and override the signals that come from our inner-heart, the place where our true self, our Soul, resides. In this way we allow ourselves to be fed by the outer world of ideals, beliefs and images rather than live true to the essence."[18]

➤ Clairvoyant (clear vision)
When people use their clairvoyant senses, they get intuitive information from visual image such as colors, pictures, symbols, or moving pictures—as if they are watching a short television clip in their head. As we learn from the Clairvoyant Center of Hawaii, "Clairvoyance works with your Spiritual Eye, rather than the physical eyes. The spiritual eye is the 6th Chakra, or Third Eye, and it is an energy center in the mid-brain, behind the forehead."[19] Children who use their clairvoyant intuition may report having vivid dreams, may see visions of lights or twinkling lights in front of their eyes, may see other people's auras, and may have imaginary friends. They will also present as being very creative.

---

[17] Anthon St. Maarten, "Claircognizance - the Gift of Psychic Knowing," LinkedIn, February 6, 2021, https://www.linkedin.com/pulse/claircognizance-gift-psychic-knowing-anthon-st-maarten.

[18] Liane Mandalis and Childcare worker, "Clairsentience," Unimed Living, Accessed September 26, 2021, https://www.unimedliving.com/unimedpedia/word-index/unimedpedia-clairsentience.html.

[19] "What Is Clairvoyance?," Clairvoyant Center of Hawaii, October 29, 2020, https://clairvoyanthawaii.com/what-is-clairvoyance/?cn-reloaded=1.

➤ Clairaudience (clear audio/hearing)
People who use this sense perceive sounds, words, or extrasensory noise. Where do these sounds come from? They can come from the spiritual world or from the ethereal realm. How are they perceived? Such sounds may be experienced as inner ear reception or as mental impressions. Clairaudient abilities can vary—clairaudients may hear the familiar voices of passed family members, may hear footsteps when no one is around, or may hear sounds that do not appear to be human. Others may experience intermittent ringing or buzzing in their ears or hear chimes or bells with no apparent source. Parents may witness their children having conversations with themselves or with an imaginary friend. Sometimes, dream discussions occur when the recipient is sleeping. Psychic children may not like to sleep alone because they are afraid of the different things they hear. Sometimes, if a child has not yet come to terms with their psychic awareness, episodes of clairaudience can terrify them—and sometimes, clairaudients can be diagnosed (wrongly) as experiencing psychosis or schizophrenia.

➤ Clairscent (clear smelling):
Do you remember how your mother's favorite perfume smelled? How your father smelled after smoking a cigarette? How your grandmother's home-baked cookies smelled? When people use their clairscent, they are tapping into energies and frequencies outside their physical surroundings. In her article "Beginners Guide to Clairalience," psychic Alissa Monroe explains clairscent in this way:

> Unlike physical senses, your psychic senses will operate using a spiritual vibration. The aromas will be brought forth straight from otherworldly realms, memories, visions, and spirits. The entire Universe and everything in it resonate using energy frequencies, and your sense of smell is no exception.[20]

When a medium contacts the spiritual world, they use their clairscent to bring through a memory for the sitter. For example, if a medium smells a wet dog, they may come into contact with a dog that has passed on. Or, if a medium smells cigar smoke, a deceased grandfather might want to connect with the sitter. Just as it is not uncommon for the aroma of our favorite foods to spark a memory from a deceased love one, the smells a medium experiences during a reading can help them connect to a spirit communicator. Not only can clairscent bring vivid, happy memories of a loved one who has passed, it can also convey a warning. For example, if a medium smells sulfur or something rotten during a reading, their clairscent might be trying to warn their sitter that a dark entity is nearby.

---

20 Alissa Monroe, "Beginner's Guide to Clairalience – the Psychic Gift of Smelling Spirits," *Psychics 4 Today*, Accessed September 26, 2021, https://www.psychics4today.com/paranormal-smells/.

➤ Clairgustance (clear tasting)
Do you remember how your grandmother's cookies tasted? How your grandpa always used to give you a special licorice candy? How the berries in your grandmother's garden tasted? Clairgustance is the sensation of tasting something when you have nothing in your mouth. Clairgustance is not just limited to the taste of food or drinks, however. With clairgustance, you might sense how a tree, a flower, an object, or a place might taste. Depending on the memory this sense provokes, it might trigger different emotions and feelings. For example, when you ate your grandmother's cookies, where were you? Tasting Grandma's cookies may relate not only to the memory of your grandmother but also to the places you went together. So, clairgustance is an amazing sense that can help a medium bring through beautiful recollections of a loved one's life and experiences.

Clairgustance can serve mediums in other ways as well. In her article "Different Modes of Sensing," Becca Nielsen, an energy medicine practitioner, says that "Sensitive people or Psychics who work in law-enforcement or forensics, for example, benefit greatly from their ability to become aware of the bitter taste of chemicals, poisons, drugs, or the iron-rich tang of blood. It often provides clues to how a victim may have been harmed/died or help solve a crime."[21]

➤ Clairtangency (clear touching)
Energy from events and people can be recorded in objects, places, and buildings. Our auras carry our personal information, and our energetic imprint remains on everything we come into contact with. Sensitives with a strong clairtangence gift can receive detailed information by touching people and objects—and if they are very sensitive, they cannot wear other people's clothing, sleep in another person's bed, or stay in a small, cluttered space because of the energy others have left on objects.

➤ Clairempathy (clear emotional feeling)
Empaths are sensitive to the energetic vibrations of others' emotions and physical illnesses; they feel others' feelings and symptoms as if they were their own. For these sensitives, being in crowded places can lead to sensory or emotional overload. Intuitives with strong clairempathy may be told that they are "overly emotional" or "too sensitive." Feeling others' negative feelings may cause sensitives to prioritize others' needs over their own and to protect themselves by becoming people pleasers. Clairempaths can attract narcissists, and peers may bully or abuse clairempathic children. Every clairempath must develop protective boundaries as a survival tool. Spending time with animals and nature can replenish a clairempath's energy.

---

[21] Becca Nielsen, "Different Modes of Sensing - Part 6: Clairgustance," Core Potentials, October 29, 2020, https://www.corepotentials.ca/blog/different-modes-sensing-clairgustance.

5. The Chakras

Writer Gretchen Stelter, an expert in yoga, tells us in her article "A Beginner's Guide to 7 Chakras and Their Meaning," that "Chakra means wheel and refers to energy points in your body. [The chakras] are spinning disks of energy that should stay open and aligned, as they correspond to bundles of nerves, major organs, and areas of our energetic body that affect our emotional and physical well-being."[22] The energy in each chakra moves clockwise and spins energy out of our body into the space around us.

It is vital to teach children about the chakras, so they understand how energy systems work and how energy flows through their physical bodies. For example, if a child's root chakra is unbalanced, they may feel fearful or may experience diarrhea or constipation. They may become under- or overweight, or they may complain of aches and pains and not feel well. When psychic children trust their intuitive senses, they will know which of their chakras are flowing with energy and which chakras are blocked and will be able to communicate this to their parents.

Every seven years, our consciousness goes through spiritual development connected to our chakras. As we begin a new stage, our soul may feel a crisis coming and because of our fear of change, we will need courage to continue our spiritual journey. According to the philosophy of the Vedic Treatise Chakravidya, we move through seven-year cycles of each chakra center. Each cycle begins with the root chakra (fear) and ends with the crown chakra (spirituality). Thus, in the first cycle, for example (ages one to seven), a child would move through each of the seven chakras noted below. In one-year phases, the child would experience the emotional and physical influences that each of the chakras govern. The main goals of the first cycle are:

➤ to learn what you want or don't want,
➤ to socialize with others,
➤ to understand the world,
➤ to discover the world,
➤ to understand how others learn from you, and
➤ to begin to explore things that are unknown to you.

---

[22] Gretchen Stelter, "Chakras: A Beginner's Guide to the 7 Chakras," Healthline Media, December 19, 2016, https://www.healthline.com/health/fitness-exercise/7-chakras#Chakra-101.

Chakras: Vedic Treatise Chakravidya Philosophy

The first cycle (ages 1-7) a child will go through the following cycles with the dominate chakra being FEAR (Root Chakra)

- Age 1: Fear + Fear (root chakra + root chakra)
- Age 2: Fear + Feelings (root chakra + sacral chakra)
- Age 3: Fear + Proactivity (root chakra + solar plexus chakra)
- Age 4: Fear + Harmony (root chakra + heart chakra)
- Age 5: Fear + Philosophy (root chakra + throat chakra)
- Age 6: Fear + Wisdom (root chakra + third eye chakra)
- Age 7: Fear + Spirituality (root chakra + crown chakra)

Spiritual writer Malavika Suresh explains how the seven-year chakra cycle begins: "After completing a [first] seven-year cycle, we enter the first stage of our second-year cycle. This is our *Crisis Year* since the first year of a new cycle is under the influence of the Root Chakra: Fear."[23]

➤ The Root/Base Chakra
This chakra is at the base of the spine and is represented by the color red. The root chakra influences your survival instincts and gives you determination, power, and physical strength. It develops when a child is between one and seven years of age.

➤ The Sacral/Spleen Chakra
This orange-colored chakra is in the lower abdomen, two inches below the navel. The sacral chakra connects us to others through feeling, desire, sensation, and movement. It also affects our ability to be joyful, creative, and compassionate. It governs sex and reproductive energy. It develops from the ages of eight to fourteen.

➤ The Solar Plexus Chakra
This chakra is above the navel, below the chest. It is represented by the color yellow, and gives us personal power, social identity, influence, self-control, joy, inner harmony, and inner strength. The solar plexus chakra develops from the ages of fifteen to twenty-one.

➤ The Heart Chakra
The heart chakra is at the center of the chest and is represented by the color green. The heart chakra gives us unconditional love, harmony, forgiveness, healing, compassion, understanding, personal transformation, and selflessness. It provides us with the ability to accept love from others and to give love to others. This chakra develops from the ages of twenty-one to twenty-eight.

---

[23] Malavika, "Chakras: 7 Year Development Life-Cycles," January 11, 2014, https://hellomalavika.com/2012/09/22/chakras-7-year-development-life-cycles/.

➤ The Throat Chakra

The throat chakra is in the throat area and is represented by the color blue. This chakra's function is to give voice to the heart chakra and to allow us to speak about our authentic self. It is also related to communication and creativity. The throat chakra develops between the ages of twenty-nine and thirty-five.

➤ The Third-Eye Chakra

The third-eye chakra is in the middle of the forehead between the eyes. Represented by the color indigo, the function of this chakra is to give us inner vision, intuition, clairvoyance, insight, perception, imagination, projection of will, and manifestation. Many people consider the third-eye chakra the gateway to the soul. When this chakra is open, you will experience spiritual wisdom and enlightenment. The third-eye chakra develops between the ages of thirty-six and forty-two.

➤ The Crown Chakra

The crown chakra is at the top of the head and is a mix of silver, gold, white, and violet. The feminine energy of creation is the color silver, the masculine energy of creation is gold, and truth and clarity are white/violet. We can connect with the Divine, with our higher self, and with the spiritual realm. This is the combination of All That Is and Divine connection. When we open the crown chakra, we can reach a timeless spiritual world in which we can have clarity and wisdom. The crown chakra develops between the ages of forty-three and forty-nine years of age.

6. The Aura

The aura is an electromagnetic energy field that surrounds all living beings. There are seven layers in the human aura, and these layers correlate with spiritual, physical, mental, and emotional health. Many psychic children see colors or different energies surrounding people—they are seeing the human aura. Just as people are all different, auras come in all different shapes and sizes. In her article "The 7 Layers of Your Aura," intuitive writer Tanaaz Chubb puts it succinctly: "In a healthy state, the entire aura can extend several feet and is dazzling. In an unhealthy or weakened state, the auric field can be small and dull. The layers of the aura pulsate outwards from the body."[24] Below is an outline of the layers of the auric energy field:

➤ First Layer – Etheric

This layer is nearest to the physical body and relates to the root chakra. The etheric aura represents all the systems of the physical body. Varying in color from light blue to gray, a psychic who can use clairvoyance (clear vision) may see sparks of bluish-white light moving through the etheric layer. People who have a strong etheric layer are healthy.

---

[24] Tanaaz, "The 7 Layers of Your Aura," Forever Conscious, October 10, 2020, https://foreverconscious.com/7-layers-aura.

➤ Second Layer – Emotional
This layer correlates with the sacral chakra and can be any colors of the rainbow that are like the chakra colors. Since this layer represents emotions and feelings, during stressful periods the color can become murky.

➤ Third Layer – Mental
This layer relates to the solar plexus chakra and is bright yellow. Thoughts, cognitive processes, and states of mind are associated with the mental layer of the aura. During a creative moment, sparks can emanate from this layer.

➤ Fourth Layer – Astral
This layer is connected with the heart chakra and is pink or rosy. This is the level in which we develop astral cords that connect our energy field with others'. When we nurture healthy relationships, this layer becomes stronger.

➤ Fifth Layer – Etheric Template
This layer is connected with the throat chakra and can vary in color. It is associated with the entire blueprint of your physical body on a higher spiritual plane and is your inner identity. Your soul connects with your body through the etheric template. Sound therapy is effective when healing different aspects of the etheric layer.

➤ Sixth Layer – Celestial
This layer is connected with the third eye chakra and is pearly white. It represents connection with the Divine and other beings. When someone has a strong celestial layer, they can receive messages from angels and communicate with the spiritual world.

➤ Seventh Layer – Ketheric Template
This layer is connected with the crown chakra. It is gold in color and contains information about your soul and your past lives. When this layer is strong, a person feels at one with the universe.

> ## Exercise: Other People's Auras
>
> *If a child talks about seeing colors around a person, give them a drawing of a stick figure and ask them to draw the colors they see. Or, ask the child to draw their own figure and place the colors around it. Then, you can discuss the meaning behind the different colors by asking the child what he or she feels the colors convey about the person.*
>
> *In her article "Many Children See Auras," life coach and inspirational speaker Cynthia Sue Larson explains that, "While young children may not yet be able to describe the fullness of perception they experience with their beginner's minds, they can convey some of their auric perceptions through art."[25]*

7. Spirit Guides
    Everything in the universe is energy, and everything vibrates at a different frequency. Since we live in the physical world, we have a lower vibration rate than that of entities that do not occupy the physical realm. In Western spiritualist cultures, spirit guides are reincarnated spirits who have agreed to work with living individuals as they fulfill their soul's path. As an article on the Lifestyle blog at *typicallytopical.com* tells us, the term "spirit guide," "…is a general term that covers all types of guides including, but not limited to; guardian angels, archangels, ascended masters, enlightened beings, starseeds, shamans, goddesses and more."[26]

    ➤ Angels
    Many young children have visits from angels. These children describe having seen bright light and colors, having felt a loving energy around them, and having felt safe. Frequently, children see angels in human form. Angelic guides are protectors and messengers, with high, pure vibrations—they have not walked in human form on the earth plane. Each one of us has a guardian angel who stays with us throughout our lifetime.

    ➤ Ascended Masters
    Jesus Christ, Mother Mary, the Buddha, and other spiritual teachers and healers who have walked the earth plane are known as Ascended Masters. During their lifetimes, they completed their own soul contract or the Divine's plan for them. Having gained supreme knowledge and wisdom from their life experience, they dwell in another, higher realm and serve as teachers of humanity in order that all souls may ascend. Some fortunate human beings (including gifted psychic children) have met with these

---

[25] Cynthia Sue Larson, "Many Children See Auras," Reality Shifters, Accessed September 26, 2021, http://realityshifters.com/pages/articles/childrenseeauras.html.

[26] "The 11 Most Powerful Types of Spirit Guides on Your Team," Typically Topical, September 4, 2021, https://typicallytopical.com/types-of-spirit-guides/.

masters while on the physical plane. For example, Christina Pierson, author of *A Knowing: Living with Psychic Children*, discusses how her son told her that before he was born he had visited Jesus, and that he missed seeing him. When he was four years old, her son drew a picture of Jesus.

➤ Elders

Just as we all have spirit guides that walk with us during our lifetimes, we also have elder guides. These guides understand your soul's life contract, helped you script the lessons you learned during your life on Earth, chose spirit guides for your team, and selected the souls whose lives will intertwine with yours during your life's journey. You will have the same elder guide throughout your lifetime.

➤ Master Guide

You may have lived many lifetimes with your master guide. Based on your spiritual lessons, you chose the ideal master guide to help you achieve and learn your lessons. Your master guide will never decide anything for you, but they will be there to assist you on your journey.

➤ Your Higher Self

This is the part of you that is connected to the Divine. When you use your intuition as a tool to tap into Your Higher Self, you can gain sacred knowledge and wisdom and advance on your spiritual path.

➤ Spirit Animal Guides

Spirit guides that show themselves as animals are connected to the energy of earth and they offer guidance and protection. A spirit animal guide may represent your personality. For example, if you have a large physique and a gentle personality, but know how to stand up for yourself, your spirit animal might be a bear. Like other guides, spirit animal guides are ascended beings and vibrate at a higher frequency than human beings.

Is it possible that your child's imaginary friend is a spirit guide? Psychology Professor Tobin Hart and his colleague Erin E. Zellars researched this topic, and documented their findings in an article, "When Imaginary Companions are Sources of Wisdom":

We have come across many accounts of what we might label guides, or ghosts. This evidence pushes the edge of conventional psychological explanation, and while one may dismiss this as fantasy or interpretive naivete, science suggests that the different nature of this material warrants further inspection.[27]

---

[27] T. Hart and Erin E. Zellars, "[Pdf] When Imaginary Companions Are Sources of Wisdom: Semantic Scholar," January 1, 1970, https://www.semanticscholar.org/paper/When-Imaginary-Companions-Are-Sources-of-Wisdom-Hart-Zellars/2107369fa6d900bce4b34bc4bb71acdbc1c9dd0a.

All the people Hart and Zellars interviewed described their childhood imaginary friends. These imaginary friends brought comfort, love, and important messages, and the individuals interviewed stated that they connected with their imaginary friends via a shift in consciousness. For example, people who meditate learn to clear their minds and shift their awareness away from the physical world and to listen and connect with the spiritual world. When children connect with their imaginary friends, they too are connecting with the spirit world. It is easier for children to connect with the other, higher realms because they do not have the everyday distractions adults have. Parents should feel at ease when they discover their child has an imaginary friend, especially when this imaginary friend gives their child companionship and comfort. Parents who are inquisitive about their child's imaginary friend may ask their child to ask their friend, "Why are you here?"

4

Focusing on Energy

Yoga, Breathing, Working with Energy, and Meditation

Yoga

Practicing yoga has many physical benefits. When children learn yoga poses, they learn to feel different energies, to ground themselves, to balance their chakras, and to breathe. Children who experience anxiety or low self-esteem; who have difficulty concentrating or poor memory; who are impulsive; or who have difficulty regulating their emotions will all benefit from a yoga routine.

Instructors who teach children yoga should incorporate imagination, music, drawing, and storytelling into their yoga routines. In her 2007 *Yoga Journal* article, "Why Kids Need Yoga as Much as We do," yoga instructor Marsha Wenig explains that "We used the yoga asanas as a springboard for exploration of many other areas—animal adaptations and behavior, music and playing instruments, storytelling, drawing—and our time together became a truly interdisciplinary approach to learning."[28] Wenig suggests, for example, that if you do the downward-dog yoga pose with children and ask them to bark like a dog, or if they complete the cobra pose and you have them hiss like a cobra, the auditory element augments the energy release. Associating stories with different poses will create a purpose for the pose. While children are in the tree yoga pose, for example, instructors can ask them to pretend they are a tree with roots going deep into the ground. Giselle Shardlow at Kids Yoga Stories has developed a program that integrates Chakra Yoga poses that include a positive affirmation with each chakra.[29]

1. Root Chakra
   Children complete the Tree yoga pose and say the affirmation, "I am secure."

---

[28] Marsha Wenig, "Why Kids Need Yoga as Much as We Do," Yoga Journal, September 2, 2021, https://www.yogajournal.com/teach/teaching-methods/yoga-for-kids/.

[29] Shardlow , Giselle, "Chakras for Kids: Learn about Their Emotions through Yoga Poses for Kids," Kids Yoga Stories, Yoga and mindfulness resources for kids, April 20, 2020, https://www.kidsyogastories.com/chakras-for-kids/.

2. Sacral/Spleen Chakra
   Children finish the Warrior 2 pose and then affirm,
   "I enjoy my life."

3. Solar Plexus Chakra
   Children complete the Half Moon yoga pose and
   say, "I am confident."

4. Heart Chakra
   Children finish the Puppy yoga pose and state,
   "I am kind."

5. Throat Chakra
   Children complete the Bridge yoga pose and say,
   "I am creative."

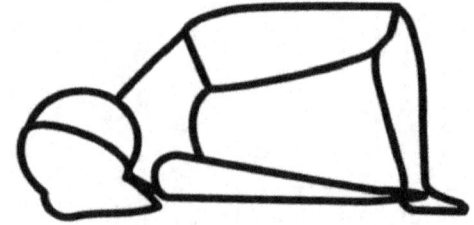

6. Third Eye Chakra
   Children finish Legs on the Wall yoga pose and state, "I am open-minded."

7. Crown Chakra
   Children complete the Resting yoga pose and say, "I am peaceful."[30]

Depending on the needs of the child you are working with, you can create your own yoga program with different poses and affirmations.

Breathing Techniques

When something frightens us or makes us anxious, our natural fight-or-flight instincts are to stop breathing, freeze, or run away. Breathing techniques can calm and center children who are nervous, restless, or fearful. Once psychic children learn these breathing techniques and use them, whenever a supernatural event arises they can respond by using their favorite breathing technique to calm themselves down.

You can teach these breathing techniques to children as they complete yoga poses, or you can use bubbles, a feather, or a pinwheel to augment the breathing method. Giselle Shardlow, the founder of Kids Yoga Stories, has developed several breathing exercises for children that you will find helpful.[31]

---

[30] Shardlow, 2020
[31] Giselle Shardlow, "5 Breathing Exercises for Kids for Calm and Focus (+ Free Poster)," Kids Yoga Stories, Yoga and mindfulness resources for kids, January 18, 2021, https://www.kidsyogastories.com/breathing-exercises-for-kids/.

1. Loving Kindness Breath
   Children should sit in a chair or on the floor. Have them tune into their breathing, take a deep breath, and release the breath in five counts. During the next exhale, have them think of filling themselves with love and imagining the color red spreading through their bodies. On the next exhale, have them send love and kindness to someone they know. Then, on the next exhale, ask them to send love to someone that they are having a difficult relationship with. On the final exhale, ask them to send love to the world that surrounds them, including the animals, plants, and people in their community.

2. Woodchopper Breath
   Children should stand tall in the mountain yoga pose and take a few breaths. Then, have them spread their feet wide, clasp their hands together in front of their body, and lift their hands, arms straight, above their heads. They should take a deep breath, and as they exhale with their mouth open, they should bend down and swing their hands between their legs. While bending down, they should release all tension from their bodies. Tell them to pretend to be a woodchopper, chopping wood for a fire. Repeat as many times as needed to release stress and extra energy.

3. Bee Breath

This exercise should begin when the children are sitting with a tall spine, shoulders back. Ask them to close their eyes and take a few breaths to calm and center their body. They should breathe through their noses; their mouths should be closed. As they exhale, tell them to make an "mmmm" buzzing sound—they can imagine they are a bee flying through flowers. They can cup their ears with their hands to get a louder audio effect.

4. Deep Belly Breath

The Deep Breath[32] exercise is also known as Yogic breathing or Pranayama which is the foundation of yoga practice. The children need to get into a comfortable upright position in a chair or on the floor. They may choose to lie on their back in a resting position or may sit up. As the children complete this Deep Belly Breath exercise, they can think of things they are grateful for.

Ask the children to place their right hand on their belly and their left hand on their chest. Then, ask them to take a deep breath while counting to four, and to exhale through their nose while counting to four. Their lips should be closed. Ask them to feel—and concentrate on—the rising and falling motion of their belly and chest during the exercise. If they are lying on their backs, they can place a stuffed animal on their belly so they can watch the animal move up and down with the rhythm of their breath.

---

[32] Deep Belly Breath – Caution: This is a powerful breathing exercise and may trigger traumatized children.

5. Flower Breath

This exercise teaches children how to become aware of their breath. Children should find a comfortable sitting position, then close their eyes and tune into their breath. Ask them to imagine they are holding a flower, and to visualize the flower's color. Ask, "How does the flower smell?" As they take a deep breath in, ask them to pretend they are smelling the flower. As they exhale, ask them to pretend to blow the flower petals away. Or, you could ask the children to pretend they are drinking a cup of hot chocolate. As they breathe in, ask them, "How does the hot chocolate smell?" As they breathe out, ask them to imagine cooling the hot chocolate down by blowing on it.

6. Kinesthetic Breathing Techniques

In learning how to control their breathing during stressful events, some children may need to use kinesthetic breathing techniques, just as dancers develop muscle memory when completing the sequence of dance movements. Here are a few techniques to help:

a) The Hoberman Sphere

Engineer Chuck Hoberman created the Hoberman Sphere in 1990, and his design was used to create a plastic toy which became popular among children. Children can unfold, expand, and contract the ball. As they breathe in, they can expand the ball outward and, as they breathe out, they can push the ball inward. This illustrates what is happening to their chest wall as they breathe in and out.

b) Bubbles

While blowing on the bubble wand, children learn how to regulate their breathing by expanding their breath from a gentle breath to deep breath.

c) Using Different Shapes with Directions

Using the drawings below, you can ask the children to follow the directions as they follow the shape. (You can use different shapes with each set of breathing directions).

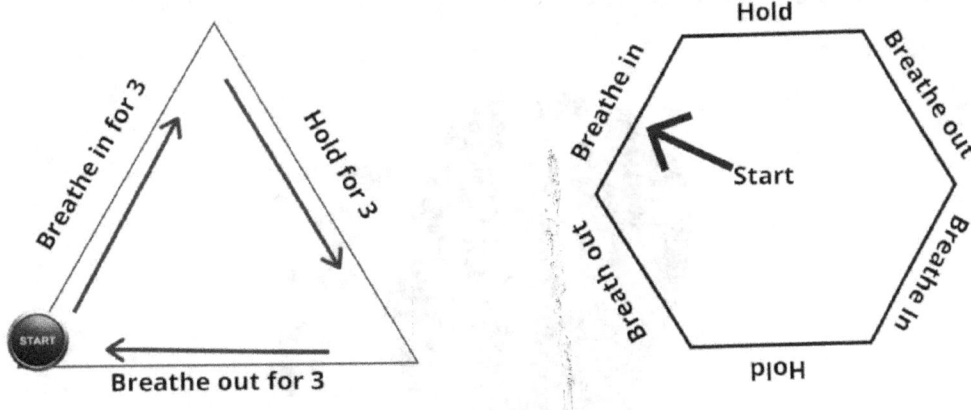

d) Straw Breathing

Give the children a straw to place in their mouths. Have them suck in, then ask them to breathe out through the straw. This exercise teaches them to use their diaphragm to breathe.

e) Ocean Breathing
Ask the children to imagine an ocean wave rolling toward them as they breathe in. As they breathe out, ask them to imagine the ocean waves rolling out to sea.

f) Color Breathing
As the children take a breath in, ask them to imagine a beautiful color that represents happiness, joy, and calmness filling their lungs. As they breathe out, ask them to imagine a color that represents stress, anxiety, or fear leaving their bodies.

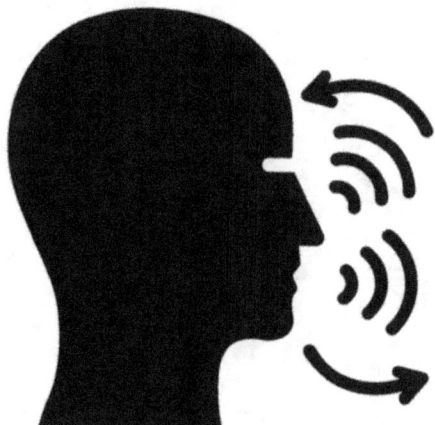

Energy Ball / Chi Ball

When psychic children feel energy around them, creating an energy ball will empower them. To create an energy ball, children should sit in a comfortable position. They will need to take a few deep breaths to relax and calm their minds.

When they are ready, first ask them to rub their palms together and then to pull their palms apart. Then, ask them to bring their palms together again. When their palms are nearly touching, they should feel a small energy resistance. Have them do this a few times until they feel this energy resistance. Then they can create their energy ball.

Ask them to make the ball a certain color; they can choose the color intuitively. They should vocalize their intention for the energy ball. "I give myself love, and I am grateful for_____."

After the children voice an intention, ask them to imagine placing the energy ball in their heart.

The children can also create an energy ball for someone else—they can send the ball to someone who needs love and healing. Then, their intention may change to, for example, "I give you love."

Meditation

After the children learn different breathing techniques, it will be easier to teach them how to meditate. When practiced regularly, meditation has many benefits, including reducing stress and anxiety, improving self-esteem, increasing focus and concentration, and promoting better sleeping patterns.

Meditation lessons can start as early as the toddler stage. You can teach a toddler to breathe in and out for thirty seconds as he or she closes their eyes. When a child is between three and six years old, you can help them meditate by telling them a story as they lie down. You can play recorded, guided meditations to a child when they reach the age of seven. At age twelve, you can add music to the meditation.

As a general guideline, a child can meditate for one minute per age. So, for example, a seven-year-old might be able to meditate for seven minutes.

The best way to teach a child why meditation is important—and the benefits of meditation—is through parental modeling. If parents meditate daily, their children will follow their example.

Exercise: Mandala Doodle

Using the concept of drawing a mandala, you can teach a child how to create spirit art. The word mandala in Sanskrit means "circle," and the mandala doodle starts by drawing a circle. Once a child draws a circle, he or she should write a word or an intention in the middle of the circle. Then, using differently colored markers, the child can draw more circles around the main circle. Then, the child can add geometric shapes, pictures, or doodles to the rest of the page as he or she ponders the words in the circle.

Young artists can ask questions about the words and allow their hands to be guided as they draw. Here is an example of what a finished mandala doodling artwork might look like.

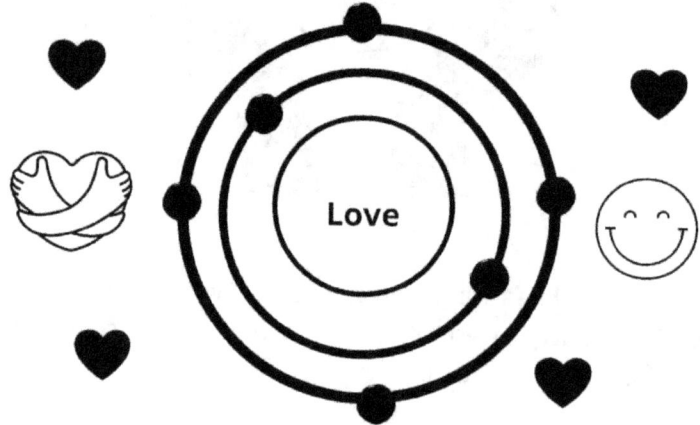

5
Feeling in Control

Protection and Being in Control

Children who are intuitive give off a light energy that attracts all spirits—even the scary ones. So, when children are visited by spirits (including loved ones who have crossed over), it can be a frightening experience. It is important for these children to know that *they are in control of how they handle spiritual situations*. It is vital that they learn to set boundaries, not only for spirit visitors but also for spirit guides and angels. Most practicing psychics or professional mediums set these boundaries—as with any job, psychic mediums establish that there are certain hours they work, and in the other hours they live their normal lives.

If a child wants a spirit to leave, he or she needs to state in a firm tone, "Please leave." There are rituals that a child can perform not only to set boundaries, but to compel a spirit to leave a house or a person's energy field. Below is a list of simple rituals you can make part of your family's spiritual routine. Remember, you need to choose rituals and customize them for your family unit. Every family is unique and not every ritual will be a comfortable fit. It is essential that a child completes the rituals with their parents.

Smudging

You can use sage or palo santo to create smoke for smudging. Establish your intention for the cleansing ritual before you begin. Always start at your front door. Work through your home clockwise, remembering to smudge inside closets and in tight spaces. As you walk around the house, chant an intention, a mantra, or a prayer. As you approach your front door again, complete the smudge ceremony by visualizing bright light engulfing your house. State your intention one last time by using your prayer or mantra. For an hour after the ceremony, leave your doors or windows open. This will allow the energy you do not want in your home to depart.

Crystals

Each crystal has a different frequency that helps positive, healing energy flow through our bodies and clear out negative or toxic energy that may harm us. Intuitive people wear crystals as a charm to protect themselves or their homes. People choose their own crystals, and children should be no exception. When you are next in a crystal store, allow your child to peruse a collection of crystals you can afford to purchase, and let them choose the one that resonates with them. They will feel more secure and in control if they connect with the crystal they wear. Below are some characteristics and properties of powerful crystals that can benefit your psychic child.

Amethyst:

This crystal is connected to the third eye and the crown chakra, and it strengthens your intuition and psychic abilities. It radiates calming energy. By wearing an amethyst, a child will be able to tune into messages sent from the spiritual world. Children are drawn to amethyst because of its vibrant purple tones.

Azurite:

If a child has an imaginary friend or connects with his or her spirit guides, archangels, or ascended masters, azurite may be beneficial. It is a powerful third-eye crystal that keeps the pineal gland from getting blocked with calcium deposits. Placing the azurite where the third eye chakra is located (between the eyes) will prevent the blockage. Azurite is also known to assist with personal growth and to increase the wearer's spiritual connection to Earth.

Charoite:

This crystal generates an auric shield for psychic protection. When children receive messages from the spiritual world, charoite will comfort them, and they will feel that their angels and guides are with them. Crystal experts have reported that charoite can be beneficial for autistic children. Since these children are known to exhibit obsessive and anxious behaviors, charoite will help them feel empowered and grounded.

Labradorite:

Children are drawn to labradorite because of its playful energy and shimmering colors. Labradorite will keep the aura healthy and the chakras aligned and open. When children are talking to spirit guides, angels, or fairies, this crystal will enhance the clarity of the messages received. When children are facing negative energies, labradorite will help them feel self-confident. This crystal also strengthens children's immune systems.

Clear Quartz:

This crystal draws positive thoughts and energy from others, and it helps manifest these thoughts into existence. When children are learning how to manifest things they desire, they can make wishes while holding this stone. Clear quartz can help children understand not only that the universe listens to our wishes, but that it also takes time for a desired situation or thing to manifest in physical form.

Tiger's Eye:

Children with intuitive abilities enjoy daydreaming, and the tiger's eye stone helps center and ground them. It assists with improving self-esteem, strengthening intuition, and motivating the wearer to live with integrity. This crystal protects travelers.

Crystal Clearing – The Salt and Water Bowl Technique

If a psychic child feels there is an unwelcome spirit in the house, this technique can cleanse the house of unwanted energy. You should only perform this technique at night, and the child should be present and be a part of the cleansing.

For this clearing ritual, you will need a white bowl that is approximately seven inches in diameter, one-quarter cup of sea salt, and a jar in which you have left black tourmaline crystals soaking in two cups of purified water for twenty-four to forty-eight hours (during which time the crystal will charge the water with positive and protective energy).

First, pour the sea salt into the bowl, and as you stir the sea salt with your hands, say a prayer or a mantra. Together, you and your child should state your intention: to get rid of the uninvited guest.

Pour the sea salt from the bowl into a circle on the floor. The circle should be big enough that there is room for the bowl at its center. Make sure there are no gaps in the salt around the perimeter of the circle. Place the bowl in the middle of the sea salt circle and pour the tourmaline-charged water into the bowl. Make sure you leave enough room to place more salt in the bowl. Once you pour the water into the bowl, repeat the step of stirring the water with your hands as you say a prayer or chant a mantra.

Now, pour a bit of sea salt in every corner of your house and in the closets. Afterward, put the rest of the salt in the water bowl while praying for a higher power to get rid of any unwanted energy. Then, leave the water bowl and salt circle in place.

In the morning, sweep up the sea salt circle, take the water from the water bowl, and flush it all down the toilet. Do not drop any water from the bowl or spill any of the salt.

Prayers for Protection

As noted earlier, in your professional life, you may work with families that are members of a particular religion and who practice different spiritual rituals. Prayers not only offer spiritual protection for a child and his or her family, but provide other benefits as well. Children should witness their parents praying so they will learn to dedicate themselves to incorporating prayer into their lives.

When children pray, they are reminded of the blessings the Divine has provided for them. This teaches them humility, how to be more positive and embrace their life experiences, and how to build strong relationships with others. Praying can also increase a child's focus. Quieting their mind for prayer reduces a child's stress and anxiety. Prayer helps children feel protected, which increases calmness and positive life aspects. Even when times are difficult, or bad things happen, prayer can help children discern the best actions for any situation. For example, if someone hurts a child's feelings, through prayer, children can learn how to forgive.

Forgiveness is never easy, but prayer helps children learn that not everyone is perfect—so they can find the courage to forgive someone who has treated them wrongly. Prayers can also teach children moral values such as respect, honor, justice, and honesty. Through prayer, they can learn how to respect religious doctrines, how to care for (and not hurt) others, and the importance of not stealing. They will also learn how to adjust to every situation and how to compromise. Once children develop a relationship with God, they will learn how to respect a higher power and learn that they are accountable for their own behavior—to their parents, and to God.

Here are some prayers you can use to establish a daily prayer routine. Try to read the prayers with a rhythmic tone so it is easier for the child to recite them.

Psalm 23

The Lord is my shephard: I shall not want. He makes me to lie down in green pastures: he leads me beside the still waters. He restores my soul; he leads me in the paths of righteousness for his name's sake.

Yea, though I walk through the valley of the shadow of death, I will fear no evil; for you are with me; your rod and your staff, they comfort me.

You prepare a table before me in the presence of my enemies; you anoit my head with oil; my cup runs over. Surely goodness and mercy shall follow me all the days of my life: and I will dwell in the house of the Lord forever.

Now I Lay Me Down to Sleep

Now I lay me down to sleep, I pray the Lord my soul to keep.
May God guard me through the night, and wake me with the morning's light. Amen.

Now I lay me down to sleep, I pray the Lord my soul to keep.
May the angels watch me through the night, and keep me in their blessed sight. Amen.

Now I lay me down to sleep, I pray the Lord my soul to keep.
If I should live another day, I pray the Lord to guide my way. Amen.

Holy Lord

Holy Lord, thank you for your grace.
Please help me move beyond the hurdles that trip me up,
and give me the strength and wisdom to look up and see the hope,
I run toward in Christ.
In Jesus' name, Amen.

If you have completed several of these or other techniques to get rid of unwanted spirits and they are still in your house, it is possible that your child is compelling the spirit to stay. When a child is younger, their curiosity may lead them to want a spirit to remain in the house, and if that occurs, you may need to speak with your child.

Older children may be more than curious. After they have had spiritual experiences, they may become fixated on communing with the spirit world, and, in more serious cases, may even seek out darker entities or turn to cult practices such as Satanism (the worship of Satan).[33]

Why do teenagers join cults? The reasons are as broad as the circumstances these teens find themselves in:

➤ many are searching to discover who they are,
➤ some want to find happiness,
➤ some want their peers to accept them.

When children grow up in dysfunctional families, sometimes they have to raise themselves. These children may suffer from psychological conditions such as eating disorders, mood disorders, personality disorders, or sexual disorders. They are seeking spiritual guidance, and will look in various places to find what they are looking for—and sometimes they will find their way to Satanist groups, where their social skill deficits make them easy marks. In his article "Satanism and Youth's Quest for Identity," Dr. Ahmet Guc, a religious historian, says that:

Precautions should be taken, considering the fact that young people who enter such groups are high school students; motives of sex and freedom play an important role in young people joining such groups, and the tendency to prove themselves.[34]

Sandra Lee, a journalist for *The Lewiston Tribune*, in her 1992 article, "Satanism – Some Behavior May be a Warning" advises that:

---

[33] Satanism started in the 1880s in France, England, Germany, and in the United States.
[34] Ahmet Guc, "Satanism and Youth's Quest for Identity," *The Fountain*, Accessed September 26, 2021, https://fountainmagazine.com/2004/issue-45-january-march-2004/satanism-and-youths-quest-for-identity.

During the intake for the Parent Training, it is vital to have information about a child's history of exploration into the cults. What are the signs of a child experimenting in satanism or cults? If a child participates in self-mutilation, repeated unexplained cuts or injuries, extreme opposition to traditional values, and drug use, that should be cause for concern and seeking professional guidance.[35]

According to Lee, some other behavior warnings may be:

- ➤ undergoing personality changes,
- ➤ becoming interested in different recreational experiences,
- ➤ viewing only the bad things that happen in the world,
- ➤ wearing black,
- ➤ developing an obsession with death (including suicide, homicide, and the sacrificing of animals),
- ➤ becoming involved with drugs or alcohol,
- ➤ being fascinated with fire,
- ➤ obsessing about sex, and
- ➤ experiencing recurring blackouts.

If you have received information from a family you are working with that their child is in a cult, and/or has been displaying disturbing behavior, you may need to provide the family with resources to help them through the situation. Be sure you have professional tools, referral material, and background information on hand—you may not be the right person to help in this family situation.

---

[35] Sandra L. Lee, "Satanism- Some Behaviors May Be a Warning," *The Lewiston Tribune*, June 7, 1992, https://lmtribune.com/northwest/satanism-some-behaviors-may-be-a-warning/article_416eb070-a314-5866-9be9-3a1976fd5638.html.

Exercise: Creating Psychic Art Through Paint

The goal for this exercise is to teach children to trust their intuition and to strengthen their imagination. For this exercise, children will need a variety of colors of acrylic paint (seven fluid ounces is ideal), several different sizes of paint brushes, one 9 x 12" watercolor (or other wet media) paper, and a 4 x 4" piece of clear cellophane wrap.

To begin the exercise, the children should sit with their eyes closed and set an intention. They can even ask a question as simple as, "What do I want to learn from this painting?" After a few minutes, and with their eyes still closed, they need to place one hand over the different tubes of acrylic paint and pick up a tube they feel is the correct color. Holding the tube in their hands, they should open the tube of paint and squeeze a small amount into the middle of the canvas. Then, they should place the cellophane wrap over the paint and, with their eyes closed, place their fingers on top of the cellophane wrap and move the paint around on the canvas.

When they feel they are done moving the paint around, they can open their eyes and remove the cellophane wrap. Then, they need to analyze the shape of the paint and decide what type of picture they can paint from the paint blot.

They can add anything they like to the painting—they may paint an abstract, a landscape, or a portrait. When the painting is complete, they need to revisit their intention and analyze the colors, symbols, and shapes in the painting. They should ask themselves: "Did I get answers to my questions? What does this painting mean to me?"

6
Expanding Intuitive Abilities Through Art

Understanding Intuitive Abilities Through Art

Art allows children to express themselves while they are becoming aware of the world around them. If a child is dealing with an emotional or scary situation, taking part in an art activity will help them work through the situation while using all their senses. In her paper "Children, Intuitive Knowledge & Philosophy," Dr. Maria daVenza Tillmans tells us that:

> Because young children have not yet developed the cognitive skills to express themselves, they use imagination, and they rely on it to convey their understanding of the world. Imagination is the language of intuitive knowledge, borne out of our unlearnt relationship with the world.[36]

Intuitive children can use different art modalities to express what they have seen, heard, and felt while connecting with the spiritual world. When they can express themselves, these children will also benefit from increased self-esteem.

When a psychic child makes art, they will tap into their visual, auditory, and kinesthetic awareness to draw what they perceive with their clair senses. Below is a listing of some of the images, figures, designs, depictions, and story elements that may arise in psychic children's artwork.

1. Color Dictionary
    When children color, they increase their self-awareness, their independence, and, most of all, their self-expression. It is always a delight to watch small children as they try to color on the walls (much to their parents' dismay).

    Creating a color dictionary is important for children with developing intuitive abilities. What does each color represent for the child? What feelings does each color represent? As each child has a distinct personality and deals with his or her surroundings uniquely, each boy or girl may have different interpretations of colors. Here are some interpretations of colors that children might use when they draw.

---

[36] Maria daVenza Tillmans, "Children, Intuitive Knowledge & Philosophy," *Philosophy Now: a magazine of ideas*, Accessed September 26, 2021, https://philosophynow.org/issues/119/Children_Intuitive_Knowledge_and_Philosophy.

➤ Blue:
This color correlates with calmness, wellbeing, and relaxation. Children who are calm and have a timid personality may enjoy creating with this color. Blue can also mean stability, strength, trust, peace, loyalty, and integrity. It is also used to depict water, the ocean, and the sky.

➤ Red:
If children use this color frequently, it may show that they are suppressing anger. If they use red moderately, it may show that they are energetic. Red can also have different meanings, including power, authority, prosperity, and joy. Many individuals who are extroverts may prefer to wear red.

➤ Black:
Many people believe that using the color black shows that a child may have a negative personality, or that the child is depressed. But art therapists believe it is just the opposite—children who use the color black may in fact have strong self-esteem and self-confidence. The color black can also represent stability, strength, darkness, evil, death, or sorrow.

➤ Yellow:
This color illustrates happiness and joy in children. Yellow may also mean intellect, optimism, cheerfulness, impatience, a critical nature, or cowardice.

➤ Green:
If children use this color too much, it may show that they are lazy or shy. Green can also mean wellbeing, growth, balance, positive self-reliance, possessiveness, envy, or sickness. It may also represent money.

➤ Purple:
If a child uses this color, they may feel sad, dissatisfied, or restless. The color purple can also represent creativity, immaturity, impracticality, imagination, magic, mystery, and royalty.

➤ Orange:
Children who use orange may be emotionally strong and enthusiastic. This color can also mean communication, optimism, pessimism, or superficiality.

Interpreting the pictures a child draws and the colors they use will be easier once you have a representation of what each color means to that child. When creating a color dictionary with a child, have them draw things he or she thinks represents those colors. You can also use pictures from the internet or magazines.

2. Different Forms of Spirit Art

Fred Rogers, American author and host of the children's television program, *Mister Rogers' Neighborhood*, once stated that, "When children pretend, they are using their imaginations to move beyond the bounds of reality. A stick can be a magic wand. A sock can be a puppet. A small child can be a superhero."[37] Similarly, children can use different art medias to connect with the spiritual world. They may not be aware that they are connecting with spirit, however, for it is often easy for them to do so. Akiane Kramarik, a young American poet and painter, is a great example. Akiane began to draw when she was just four years old, and her inspiration for creating an art piece developed from when she first met God.[38] "Where God takes me," Akiane explains, "He teaches me to paint."[39] When Akiane was just five years old, she went missing from her family's home and disappeared without a trace. As the entire community looked for her, Akiane reports she was in another world, where she met God. Creating art was her way of telling the story she could not describe in words. When Akiane first painted, she used candles, fruits, vegetables, charcoal, or pencils as media to illustrate her dreams and visions. Dreams Akiane had about Jesus were her inspiration for her first masterpiece—at eight years old, she created her famous painting of Jesus, "Prince of Peace." As she paints, she feels a connection with God—and she states that there are many art pieces she has completed that she cannot understand or interpret. But when Akiane paints, she has purpose and conveys a message from the Divine. Thus, Akiane's artwork represents what we know as "spirit art." When a psychic or medium taps into the spirit world and channels that energy into developing paintings, drawings, books, symbols, music, or song lyrics, they too create spirit art. Parents can teach their children several methods of creating spirit art.

➤ Automatic Drawing

In automatic drawing, people with psychic abilities allow spirit or higher self to control their hands as they create. Artists create art pieces without conscious intention (in an awake state), or they draw in a dream state under hypnosis or in trance. During the Surrealism movement, artists would create paintings, poems, or writings by placing themselves in a dream state. In their article "Surrealist Techniques: Automatism," Dr. Charles Cramer, a professor of history, language, and global culture, and Dr. Kim Grant, a professor of art history, report that "Automatism was a group of techniques used by the Surrealists to facilitate the direct and uncontrolled outpouring of unconscious thought."[40] Andre Benton, writer and poet, completed experiments in psychic automatism in 1922. These experi-

---

[37] "50 of the Greatest and Most Inspirational Quotes About Play," Nurtured Neurons, December 26, 2020, https://www.nurturedneurons.com/quotes-about-play/.

[38] https://akiane.com/my-story/

[39] Kramarik, Akiane. *Akiane: Her Life, Her Art, Her Poetry*. Nashville: Thomas Nelson, 2017. Kindle.

[40] Charles Cramer and Kim Grant, "Surrealist Techniques: Automatism (Article)," Khan Academy, Accessed September 26, 2021, https://www.khanacademy.org/humanities/art-1010/dada-and-surrealism/xdc974a79:surrealism/a/surrealist-techniques-automatism.

ments intertwined the surrealism movement with the spiritualism movement. Women who were practicing spiritualism used automatic writing or speaking when they were connecting with the spiritual world. The techniques used during the surrealism and spiritualism movements are similar.

When automatic writing or drawing while connecting to spirit, clear your conscious mind through deep breathing. Then enter either a trance state or an awakened state without conscious thought. Allow your hand to write or draw without hesitation and let the information flow. If you are writing words, you may hear the words spoken in your head. While creating automatic drawings, the artist can also use different clairs as they draw. For example, you can intend to use your clairvoyance as you draw, and then allow that clair to guide the creation of an art piece. You will just feel or know what you need to draw. Automatic drawing should be easy for children, as they have great imaginations.

If a child you are working with is interested in practicing spirit art, doodling is a great place to start. When people doodle, they don't think, and they have no goal in mind. Many people doodle when they are at a long business meeting or on the phone, or when they are just plain bored. Below is an art exercise project a child can do when practicing automatic drawing.

Exercise: Doodle

To complete this exercise, the child will need liquid school glue, dark paper, and chalk or pastels. After he/she collects the materials, he/she needs to clear his/her mind. Ask the child to close their eyes and concentrate on their breathing for two minutes.

When they open their eyes, the child needs to pick up the liquid school glue and doodle (draw) with it. Without planning, he/she should make loops and lines and allow their hand to flow.

Let the glue dry. Once the glue is dry, using the chalk or pastels, the child should color all (or some of) the shapes they created and then blend the colors with their fingers. Bold, bright colors work best if you use black paper. When the child is done coloring, he/she can add black abstract lines or elements back into the drawing with black chalk to create contrast. The child can draw over the glue outline as well with a black marker.

Using the same doodling concept, a child can use a marker or a pencil and concentrate on making loops and straight lines on his or her drawing. The child can use different colors for contrast, or create unique pictures formed by the loops and straight lines.

> Auragraph

Older children with intuitive abilities may want to create an auragraph when they are giving others a psychic reading. Harold Sharp, a medium and spirit artist, and his spirit guide, Chin Shih, created the Auragraph below. As he was talking to his friends over the phone, Harold used to scribble on a piece of paper. Discovering that his scribbles were meaningful symbols, he incorporated this process into his mediumship sessions.

People who draw auragraphs can read other's auras, and as we saw in the topic on auras earlier, information about a person's soul is stored in levels of the aura—much like a computer chip stores an infinite amount of information. While many spirit artists follow the traditional method of drawing auragraphs in the shape of a mandala, you can use your own technique to create your auragraphs.

An auragraph is like a storyboard illustrating someone's life journey. As the child receives information about a person, he or she can begin at the bottom of the circle, drawing past events concerning a person's health; their financial and spiritual relationships; their emotional and mental wellbeing, and their fears and fantasies, hopes and dreams. Then, working around the circle clockwise, with each segment of the circle symbolizing different eras in someone's life, the child can continue to draw their impressions as they continue the reading.

A child can also create an auragraph by tapping into their intuition alone, or they can use tools (such as oracle cards, tarot cards, or Lenormand cards). If they decide to use oracle cards and they are doing an in-person reading, the child should ask their sitter to draw five cards. Then, using the template below, the child can draw symbols, colors, lines, loops, or other shapes to channel a cryptic message for the client.

Alternatively, the child can analyze the words written on the oracle card and then write their interpretation inside the circle, or they can write words that come intuitively. This type of auragraph can be created by hand or on a computer.

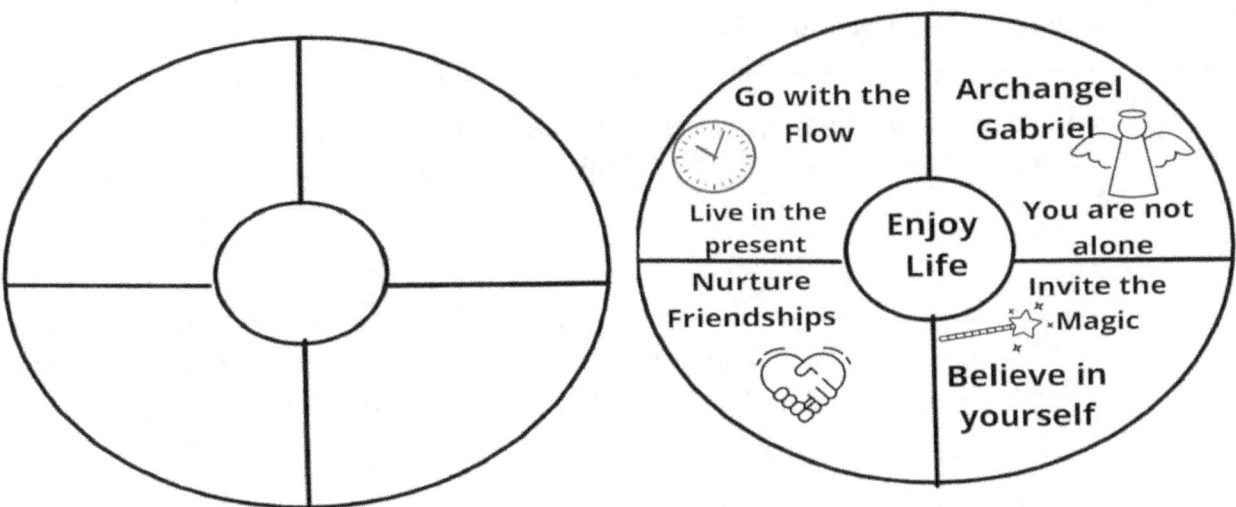

A child can create a *free-flowing auragraph* by creating a picture story without the circle boundaries as well. In this method, ask the child to divide a piece of paper into sections, showing different time lines. Alternatively, the child can create one continuous story. Adding advice or inspiration together with information received during a reading makes the auragraph more powerful to the sitter.

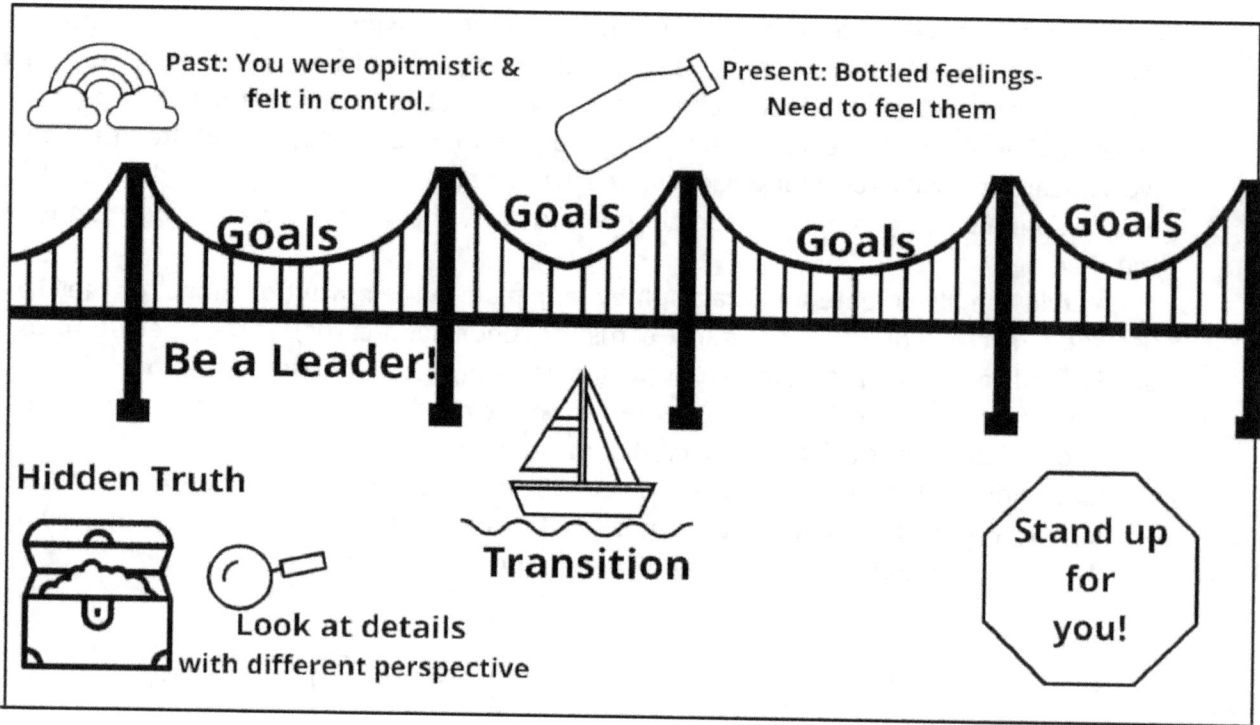

When creating an auragraph, a psychic child needs to consider adding the art elements noted below. The child should ask, "What do I intend each element of my auragraph to convey?"

➤ Shape:
What shape are you going to use? Are you going to use a geometric shape such as a square, heart, triangle, rectangle, circle, diamond, octagon, or oval? Or, are you going to use an organic shape by drawing leaves, clouds, plants, or animals?

➤ Line:
Will your lines be straight, swirly, wavy, thick, thin, zig-zag, diagonal, vertical, horizontal, curved, parallel, jagged, dotted, or dashed?

➤ Color:
Do you feel you need to use primary or secondary colors? What do these colors mean to you?

➤ Texture:
How would your drawing feel if you were going to touch it? Would it feel bumpy, prickly, sticky, wet, soft, rough, or smooth?

➤ Form:
Will you draw three-dimensional (3-D) shapes, such as a cube, cylinder, sphere, cone, prism, or a pyramid?

➤ Value:
Are you going to add shading to your drawing using black or gray? Are you going to add the color white for a lightening effect?

➤ Space:
Where are you going to place the objects in your drawing? Are you going to draw the objects large to make them appear closer to the viewer, or are you going to draw the objects small to make them appear farther away?

If younger children want to create an auragraph, they can always use stickers and crayons. When working with psychic children, invent different techniques for creating spirit art that works for your young client.

➤ Spirit Portraits:
We human beings have used art throughout history as a tool for self-expression, therapy, connecting with others, and for expressing religious beliefs or political perspectives. When a medium draws a portrait of a spirit that has crossed over, it becomes not only a validation of the afterlife but also helps loved ones left behind to heal. If a psychic child has seen a loved one that has crossed over and cannot draw the image themselves, they can direct another person to draw the image for them. You can give a child a template of a person's face and ask the child to add the physical features to the template. As the child draws, information about the spirit communicator may surface.

3. Creating Stories
When you are trying to get information about a situation, you will find brilliant success through storytelling. The child's age and his or her ability to write will determine whether you will need to transcribe what they tell you. When a child tells you about a real-life situation in a story, ask how they felt during the event. What did the event look like through the child's eyes? Discuss potential actions the child can take to make the event easier to deal with.

Many intuitive children are terrified when they experience a supernatural event. Many are afraid to talk to someone about what is happening. It can be helpful for a child to share an event through a third-person point-of-view and take themselves out of the story. To begin a story, you may wish to ask the child to draw a picture of what happened. A picture is a concrete way for a child to visualize the story before he or she adds language to the tale. Here are some questions you can ask to prompt a child to begin. Try asking open-ended questions:
➤ How did that happen?
➤ How did that make you feel?
➤ Can you tell me more about...?
➤ Where were you...?
➤ When did this take place...?
➤ What can you tell me about...?
➤ What can you/we do to make it better?

Adding artwork through painting, coloring, drawing, or other media will enhance the story—and you will get more information from the child.

4. Understanding Feelings in a Creative Way
    Many children may not be able to express how they feel. This can confuse empathic children, since they may not know where their feelings are coming from. They may wonder if they are experiencing their own emotions, or someone else's. First, teach the child about different feelings and what these emotions look and feel like. Below are different activities you can do.

Exercise: Pictures and Emotions Exercises

➤ *For younger children, picture books are a good place to start; they illustrate how a person looks when experiencing different feelings. For example, in illustrations, a person smiles when he is happy or frowns when she is sad.*

➤ *Examine unique pictures that show people in varying situations. Ask the child, "How do the people in this picture feel?" and "Why do they feel that way?"*

➤ *Television shows or movies illustrate how the characters are feeling in different scenes and watching programming is a fun way to teach a child about emotion.*

➤ *Incorporating drama when learning about feelings will allow a child not only to act like someone having a particular feeling, but they may also practice feeling the way someone else might have been feeling.*

➤ *An empath feels the emotional energy around a person. Even though an empathic child may understand non-verbal cues about people's emotions, they may still get confused about what a non-verbal cue is conveying. For example, a smile tells others you are happy—but what if you are hiding your true feelings? What if you are sad, but your non-verbal language shows that you are happy? By feeling your energy, an empath will know what you are feeling.*

As noted earlier, children can sense when a person is dangerous or should be avoided. When a child tells their parent that they are afraid of someone, parents should never ignore the child's concern. We should teach empathic children how to feel into a person's energy. Using colors is a great tool to help a child explain what feeling he or she is picking up from someone's energy. For example, they could use the color red to convey anger, or use yellow to show happiness. Ask the child, "What color are you feeling with that person's emotional energy?"

Once a child understands that people can reveal different feelings and emotions non-verbally (and through their emotional energy), it is time to teach the child what it means to be an empath. For younger children, you may need to show what it "looks like" to be an empath. For example, you could use puppets to act out a scene showing that one puppet is an empath, create a video clip that illustrates what an empath is, or create a comic book story illustrating different situations in which an empath may find himself or herself.

Empathic children need to adopt daily habits to replenish their energy. As noted earlier, to help their child diminish stress, parents can teach them mindfulness techniques such as breathing exercises, meditation, or yoga poses. Since every child is different, you may wish to seek information from local mental health care providers about unique techniques to manage juvenile stress.

Since empathic children have enormous hearts, they need to learn to say "No" and to examine and manage their feelings. They feel overwhelmed in situations, and when they pick up others' feelings, it can be difficult for them to deal with what is happening. These children may need someone to model to them what managing their feelings looks like.

One way parents can teach their empath child to live more simple lives is to help them plan daily activities. Many children take part in regular extracurricular activities. Parents need to know that empathic children can find it hard to block out the cacophony of energy and noise that occurs in busy environments. So, parents may want to schedule activities in such environments at less busy times. And, parents should always try to allocate alone time to an empathic child's schedule.

5. Drawing and Storytelling About Dreams
Parents often comment about the number of dreams their intuitive children have. Since dreams can connect psychics and intuitive channels to the spiritual world, parents should learn how to discern the difference between a regular dream and a psychic dream. While there are many types of dreams (some of these are listed below), as a general guideline, most psychic dreams are in rich colors, and dream analysts suggest that even if a psychic dream is in black and white, there will be an object or two in the dream that is in color.

➤ Precognitive Dreams
These dreams give the dreamer information about future events, and throughout history, many people have seen significant dreams in their lives before the events occurred. For example, two weeks before he was assassinated, President Abraham Lincoln had a precognitive dream. He described the dream to his family: He saw himself in a casket in the East Room of the White House. Eerily, this was the exact location where the staff placed his casket after Abraham Lincoln died.[41]

In *The Hidden Power of Your Dreams*, author, soul coach, and healer Denise Linn claims that if a dream is precognitive, the dreamer will always see a prominent, round object in the dream—objects such as a steering wheel, a ball, a round table, a round mirror, or a round picture.[42]

➤ Clairvoyant Real-Time Dreams
These dreams differ from precognitive dreams, as they are not foretelling the future, but instead have to do with what is taking place in real-time. In real-time dreams, a dreamer can experience the feelings of another person who is awake at the time the dream takes place. For example, if you took a nap while your child was at school and dreamed that he or she was crying on the playground because they were being bullied, and they came home and told you about the experience, you may have had a clairvoyant real-time dream.

➤ Telepathic Dreams
In a telepathic dream, the dreamer can communicate telepathically with another person who is awake during the time the dreamer is dreaming. For example, perhaps you had a difficult day before you went to sleep. In your dream you talked to your mother about the awful day's events, and she said, "I love you and I'll call you in the morning." Then, in the morning, the phone rings, and it's your mom. You had a telepathic dream.

➤ Dreams of Other Lifetimes
When someone dreams of another lifetime, their dream will often be comprised of a scenario featuring congruent languages and cultures that differ from the dreamer's current life. The dreamer will play the same character each time they dream this dream. By dreaming of other lifetimes, many people can heal from past traumas and become able to live their current lives with more passion and purpose.

[41] History.com Staff, "Did Abraham Lincoln Predict His Own Death?," History.com, A&E Television Network, October 31, 2012, https://www.history.com/news/did-abraham-lincoln-predict-his-own-death.
[42] Nicole Rose, "Psychic Dreams: What You Need to Know About This ESP Phenomenon," Medium, Dream Codes, August 28, 2020, https://medium.com/dream-codes/psychic-dreams-how-to-know-if-youve-had-one-f0839c5d29eb.

➤ Visitation Dreams

In visitation dreams, loved ones who have passed to the spirit world, spiritual guides or masters, or astral entities visit the dreamer. The dreamer feels powerful emotions, hears the voice of an invisible person, or receives spiritual guidance from a disembodied voice. After waking from a dream in which a spirit being or entity visited them, some dreamers may experience physical symptoms such as headaches, fatigue, trouble breathing, or a stomachache.

➤ Lucid Dreams

Children have a natural ability to experience lucid dreams, and, unlike adults, they have not adopted a limited belief system. We can compare a lucid dream to playing a video game. In lucid dreaming, aware that they are dreaming, a dreamer can control their dreams, extend a dream's boundaries, teleport to a different location, and learn skills that are impossible in "real life," such as flying. In their article "Lucid Dreaming Incidence: A Quality Effects Meta-Analysis of 50 years of Research," David Saunders et al. declare that "An estimated 55% of people have had one or more lucid dreams in their lifetimes and 23% of individuals experience lucid dreams one time a month or more."[43]

Lucid dreaming can have a powerful impact on psychic children, so it's helpful to teach them lucid dreaming techniques. There are other sleep-related phenomena it's helpful to discuss with psychic children as well, including hypnagogic sleep paralysis (in which the experiencer can have visions and hallucinations), astral traveling, out-of-body experience, and remote viewing.

If you are working with an intuitive child, there are several ways a family can embrace their child's dream experiences:

➤ Show an interest in the dream by talking to their child about it.

➤ Ask the child to work through the dream using storytelling, painting, music, and other creative means.

➤ Explain what type of dream the child is having. This may help the child feel supported and in control.

➤ Keep an extensive dream journal, adding pictures and explanations of each dream. Over time, a child can self-reflect on the recorded dreams.

---

[43] David T. Saunders, et al. "Lucid dreaming incidence: a quality effects meta-analysis of 50 years of research," Consciousness and Cognition, U.S. National Library of Medicine, Accessed September 27, 2021. https://pubmed.ncbi.nlm.nih.gov/27337287/.

7
Different Scenarios

As a lightworker helping families of psychic children, the spiritual knowledge you have gained from your life experiences will be vital in your work. The Divine, your higher self, and your spiritual team have been with you on your life's journey, and they have given you both your pleasant and difficult life situations as gifts of learning.

Frequently, spirit will bring souls together who are experiencing similar journeys. Each family you will work with will have different needs, but spirit will be there to guide you. When customizing a Family Service Plan for each family, remember, set nothing in stone. There is always room to change any program so a particular scenario works for your clients.

As noted earlier, once a plan is in place, always make sure that the family agrees to the plan—but be flexible. If you have to change a Family Service Plan, make sure the family agrees to the changes as well.

Steps in Creating a Family Service Plan for Helping Families

1. Retrieve information about why the family needs your services. (See "Intake" in Chapter 2, above.)
2. Parents complete the Intake Form. (See "Intake" in Chapter 2, above.)
3. Develop a Family Service Plan that includes the goals and techniques you will be using.
4. Determine how many sessions (and the duration of each session) per week you recommend for the family.
5. Provide the time frame of when the family services should end.
6. Develop a financial plan with the family so everyone is confident the family can cover the costs of the services.
7. At least one week before the services end, reevaluate the goals and the time frame agreed upon.
8. Decide if the family needs after-service consulting sessions. If so, determine how many consulting sessions you should complete.
9. So you can evaluate progress after each session, document data and create detailed notes about what occurred.

Below, I have shared several (fictitious) scenarios that represent situations you may face when working with families.

Scenario 1: Jackson

Jackson is five years old and lives at home with his mother (Lisa), his father (Paul), and two-year-old sister. Lisa reported that Jackson is speaking to a grandfather who passed away ten years ago, that he has an imaginary friend, and that he is afraid of an entity he "feels." Lisa completed the Intake Form and stated that Jackson's paranormal experiences:

➤ affect him moderately,
➤ stress his family minimally, and
➤ affect his social life significantly.

Jackson is exhibiting the following behavioral and emotional issues:

➤ He has an imaginary friend he plays cars with,
➤ He sees relatives who have passed (including his grandfather),
➤ He reports feeling different energies at home,
➤ He feels anxious and worried,
➤ He cries frequently,
➤ He is withdrawn,
➤ He hears voices in his mind, and
➤ He has sleep problems because spirits try to talk to him when he is in bed.

Lisa grew up in a Catholic home; Paul's family was not religious. Jackson's family are not members of a church. Lisa wants Jackson to know that there is a higher power and hopes that he finds spirituality. Jackson is not on medication, and there are no health concerns. He has difficulty making friends and other kids bully him at school. His teachers report he plays by himself. Based upon the information the family reported, it is easy to assume:

➤ Jackson is an empath, a medium, and a psychic.
➤ He uses clairsentience (clear sensation-feeling), clairvoyance (clear seeing), clairaudience (clear hearing), and clairempathy (clear emotional feeling).

We developed the following goals to help Paul and Lisa support Jackson and understand his intuitive gifts.

1. To help Jackson with his anxiety, he will:
   ➤ learn to strengthen his root chakra by doing the tree yoga pose and stating, "I am secure."
   ➤ learn breathing exercises such as blowing bubbles, blowing a pinwheel, and doing the woodchopper and deep belly breath exercises, and
   ➤ use a Hoberman sphere to practice deep breathing.

2. After Jackson learns basic breathing techniques, he will meditate for five minutes twice a day.

3. In order to feel in control when talking to spiritual entities, Jackson will:
   ➤ learn to set boundaries,
   ➤ learn how to talk to the spirit entities, so he can express when he wants to talk to them and when he does not, and so he'll know when to ask, "Why are you here?"

4. Jackson will pick out a crystal to hold or place near his bed when he goes to bed at night. For Jackson, I recommend charoite (which provides an auric shield for psychic protection) or clear quartz crystals (for making wishes to the universe).

5. Lisa and Paul should choose a brief prayer they can recite with Jackson each evening.

6. Jackson will learn how to explain each spiritual encounter to his parents through storytelling. Lisa and Paul will write each story in a special notebook for Jackson, and he will illustrate the story.

7. To identify each entity that visits Jackson (including his imaginary friend), he will draw how they looked when they appeared to him. Lisa and Paul can assist by asking him about each of the entity's physical features.

8. To understand his own and others' emotions, Lisa and Paul will read Jackson storybooks that illustrate characters expressing different emotions in a variety of situations. Since he is being bullied at school, they will also read books to him that address bullying. As he learns about emotions, he will learn not only what it means to be an empath but how to handle being an empath. Using puppets as one of the teaching methods, the lightworker will illustrate what an empath goes through daily.

9. The lightworker will show Lisa and Paul techniques that will help Jackson accept his spiritual gifts, and they will practice them with Jackson.

10. The lightworker will give Lisa and Paul:
    ➤ information to help them understand terminology that will arise when discussing and working in the spiritual realm.
    ➤ local references that offer social skill groups for younger children, counseling for children who are bullied, and yoga classes that offer services to children.

Jackson's family services will begin on June 1 and finish on October 31. His family will have two sessions per week of sixty minutes' duration. Lisa and Paul will pay on the first day of every month. If a payment is five days late, the lightworker will charge a late fee of $20.00.

Scenario 2: Emma

Emma is ten years old and lives with her mother, Jenn, and her thirteen-year-old sister. Jenn reported Emma feels spirit energy around her in different environments. When Emma feels too much energy, she says that she does not feel well; she feels dizzy. She receives information about the person who is with her—memories, current events, or information about what the person is thinking. She has always known how others feel. Emma is seeing colors around others and does not know how to deal with this. Because she feels this energy, Emma is avoiding community areas.

Jenn completed the Intake Form and reported that Emma's paranormal experiences:

➤ affect her moderately,
➤ do not affect her academic achievement,
➤ stress her family significantly, and
➤ affect her social life significantly.

Emma is exhibiting the following behavioral and emotional issues:

➤ She is anxious or worried,
➤ She feels how others are feeling,
➤ She is withdrawn or alone frequently,
➤ She knows what others are thinking,
➤ She predicts events,
➤ She feels different energies in environments,
➤ She talks about vivid dreams,
➤ She can see colors around others' bodies,
➤ She has a great imagination and is creative,
➤ She prays daily, and
➤ She has a family member who, in the past, displayed intuitive abilities (a grandmother).

Emma has been diagnosed with dyslexia. She enjoys going to school. She attends a local church with a family friend and enjoys reading and studying the Bible. Her mother, Jenn, does not attend church, but is spiritual.

Based upon the information the family reported, it is easy to assume:

➤ Emma is psychic and an empath.
➤ She uses claircognizance (clear knowing), clairsentience (clear sensation-feeling), and clair-voyance (clear vision).

We developed the following goals to help Emma's family support her and understand her intuitive gifts.

1. To help Emma with her anxiety and learn to deal with energy in different environments, Emma will practice basic yoga and breathing exercises with affirmations.

2. Emma will learn about the different chakras, and how to do chakra yoga poses.

3. Emma will use different breathing exercises, such as the loving kindness breath, the woodchopper breath, and color breathing, and will follow the directions for hexagon-shape breathing.

4. Emma will learn how to work with energy by creating the Energy ball/Chi ball.

5. Emma will pick out a crystal she is drawn to. She may choose protective crystals such as amethyst (emotional/spiritual protection), clear quartz (deflecting negativity and attracting positivity), and charoite (generates an auric shield).

6. To help Emma protect herself from energy in her environment, she will learn to practice the following exercises while she is in public places with large numbers of people:
   ➤ imagine a crystal box surrounding her, pushing the unwanted energy away, or
   ➤ create an imaginary shield (similar to a super hero shield) in front of her.

7. Emma will learn how to draw her aura energy away from others so she does not receive unwanted information.

8. Emma will learn about the different aura energy layers. Then, using a sheet of paper on which an outline of a person is drawn, she will draw the colors she sees surrounding people. She will create her own color dictionary, so that when she sees someone's aura, she will be able to discern what each color represents for her about that person.

9. To learn automatic writing or drawing, Emma will learn different ways to doodle while allowing her subconscious to emerge.

10. In order to become more self-aware and to connect with the spiritual realm, Emma will learn how to create a Mandala Doodle.

11. Since Emma has vivid dreams, she needs to begin a dream journal. She will write about her dreams and then illustrate them. To add to her dream journal, she can write her interpretations of her dreams.

12. Since Jenn and Emma both love to learn about angels, they can study angels together. This will bring Emma and her mother closer spiritually.

13. The lightworker will show Jenn the techniques that will help Emma accept her spiritual gifts, and she will practice them with Emma.

14. The lightworker will show Jenn information to help her understand the terminology that will arise when discussing and working in the spiritual realm.

15. The lightworker will give Jenn local references that offer children's yoga classes, counseling for children who feel anxious in social environments, and a service that fulfills Emma's creative talents.

Emma's family services will begin on January 1 and finish on May 31. Her family will have two sessions per week, each sixty minutes in duration. Jenn will pay on the first day of every month. If a payment is five days late, the lightworker will charge a late fee of $20.00.

Scenario 3: Madison

Madison is sixteen years old and lives with her parents, John and Mary. John and Mary report Madison has been tuned in to the spiritual world since she was born. She first communicated with deceased loved ones when she was five. Madison's cousin, Kara, died in a car accident when Madison was ten years old. They were close, and Kara's sudden passing was devastating for Madison. After the loss, Madison became curious about death and the afterlife. On the one-year anniversary of Kara's accident, Madison reported seeing an apparition of Kara in her bedroom.

Recently, Madison has started to communicate with the spirit world daily. John and Mary accept Madison's intuitive abilities, and Mary admits she shares the same abilities. The family does not discuss Madison's gifts with anyone as they are afraid of being shunned, but Madison wants to share her spiritual talents with her friends. She told her best friend, Hannah, and was surprised that Hannah told her she was afraid for her and that she should not open that door as evil entities will try to control her. Ever since Hannah rejected her, Madison has been depressed and isolates herself in her room.

Madison expresses her creativity with her digital camera and loves taking pictures in the community.

Usually, Madison wears bright, colorful clothes, but has switched to black tops. In the last two months, Madison's academic grades have dropped. Her family does not know how to help her.

John is not religious or spiritual, but Mary loves the teachings of Buddhism. The supernatural realm has always fascinated Madison.

John and Mary completed Madison's Intake Form together. They reported that Madison's intuitive abilities are affecting her spiritual, academic, family, and social stressors significantly. Madison is experiencing the following emotional and behavioral issues:

➤ She is withdrawn and is frequently alone,
➤ She has school issues,
➤ She hears voices inside her mind,
➤ She sees apparitions/ghosts,
➤ She knows what others are thinking,
➤ She feels different energies in different environments, and
➤ She has a living family member that displays psychic abilities (her mother, Mary).

Based upon the information the family reported, it is easy to assume that:

➤ Madison is a psychic medium and an empath.
➤ She uses claircognizance (clear knowing), clairsentience (clear sensation-feeling), clairvoyance (clear vision), clairaudience (clear hearing), and clairempathy (clear emotional feeling).

We developed the following goals to help John and Mary support Madison and understand her intuitive gifts. As Madison is sixteen, the lightworker will not only to talk with John and Mary, but also get permission to talk to Madison one-to-one.

1. The lightworker will interview Madison to determine what goals she wants to add to the Family Plan. Here are a few questions the lightworker will ask:
   ➤ How old were you when you realized you could talk to spirits? Can you tell me about that first experience?
   ➤ What other supernatural events have happened to you?
   ➤ Have you understood what has been happening to you?
   ➤ What have you learned about the supernatural realm?
   ➤ If you had a choice, how would you use your intuitive gifts?
   ➤ Do you consider yourself spiritual? Religious?
   ➤ What help do you need in accepting your intuitive gifts?

2. Madison will learn yoga and breathing techniques, so she will alleviate stress, clear her thoughts, feel healthier, and become more self-aware.

3. The lightworker will teach Madison about the different chakras, their functions, and how to keep them balanced.

4. Madison will learn to connect with her spirit guides by using guided meditation and will make meditation a habit and part of her daily routine. She will learn how to set boundaries with spirits by letting them know she will only communicate with them at certain times.

5. Madison will learn not to connect with other people's deceased loved ones without permission.

6. If Madison is drawn to crystals, she will learn about the different types and their functions, characteristics, and attributes.

7. Using her camera (or an art medium of her choice), Madison will develop a vision board to discover what she wants to manifest for her life's journey.

8. If Madison wants to develop her psychic and mediumship abilities, the lightworker will work with her to develop a plan. Madison will determine what tools she wants to use (such as oracle cards, tarot cards, crystals, or numerology). Since teenagers are curious about using tools such as the Ouija board, the lightworker will discuss the history and controversy surrounding the Ouija board with Madison and her parents.

9. If Madison is interested in using oracle cards, she can develop her own deck by using her camera. The lightworker will teach her the steps of developing an oracle card deck and how to use oracle cards. If she is interested, Madison could schedule a small party to do readings for others. (See also item 13. below)

10. Madison may wish to learn to incorporate spirit art into her psychic and mediumship readings.

11. It would benefit Madison to write in a journal daily.

12. Mary is interested in Buddhism. She may wish to consider teaching Madison what she is learning.

13. A discussion with Madison about friendship may be beneficial for her social wellbeing. Are the friends she is hanging out with supporting her authentic self? Do these friends exhibit good values and character traits? Can she trust them and be vulnerable around them?

14. To develop her photography skills, Madison may wish to enroll in a class that teaches photography techniques.

15. The lightworker will show John and Mary techniques to help Madison accept her spiritual gifts.

16. The lightworker will give John and Mary information to help them understand terminology that will arise when discussing and working with the spiritual realm.

17. The lightworker will give John and Mary local references for yoga classes, counselors for youths showing signs of depression, spiritual classes for youth, and photography and art classes.

Madison's family services will begin on February 1 and will finish on June 30. Her family will have two sessions per week, each sixty minutes in duration. The family will pay on the first day of every month. If a payment is five days late, the lightworker will charge a late fee of $20.00.

8
Celebrate Spiritual Growth

Receiving Support

Many children with intuitive abilities do not receive the support they need. Often, they accept their gifts and embrace their souls only when they go through spiritual-awakening events as adults.

The moments in which we question the purpose of our lives—when we ask ourselves why things happen in the world—are the same moments in which we connect with and align with the Divine. These moments define who we truly are. When we question our beliefs, we may feel disengaged from our loved ones, our religious sector, our day-to-day habits, even our hobbies. Until we accept these new thoughts, ideas, and philosophies, confusion may overwhelm our emotions. We will let go of things that no longer serve us and find a social community that has beliefs similar to ours and that accepts us for who we have become. When we accept who we are now, life becomes exceptional—we can't wait to see where our path may lead us. In this same way, if we can guide our psychic children to accept the abilities they have, embrace their authentic selves, and experience what it feels like to be in harmony with the Divine, they too will expand their intuitive abilities beyond what they ever thought possible.

*

Childhood Experiences

Peri Zarrella is an energy healer, therapeutic healer, psychic medium, and television personality who helps children on the A&E television show *Psychic Kids: Children of the Paranormal*. When Peri was eight years old, she went through a Near-Death Experience (NDE). After this incident, she heard voices, saw spirits, and received information from the spiritual world. She felt alone and overwhelmed by her new intuitive gifts, but as she got older, she accepted them—she knew she could use them to help others.

Another intuitive who helps children on *Psychic Kids* is paranormal theorist and researcher Ryan Michaels. Ryan began to have intuitive skills at age ten when he received information about people's lives and emotions clairvoyantly. At thirteen, he communicated with spirits, participated in astral projection and remote viewing, and found he could travel to locations in the past, present, and future. These paranormal experiences petrified Ryan until he realized he could use his psychic skills to help children feel safe as they began to understand their own intuitive gifts.

The list of psychics and mediums who discovered their gifts as children is astounding. Another famous medium's story comes from American author and medium Allison DuBois (on whose life the network television show *Medium* was based). When she was six years old, Allison saw her deceased grandfather at the end of her bed. He told her to tell her mother he was no longer in pain; that he was still living. When she relayed the message to her mother, she told Allison to go back to bed. After this incident, Allison kept hearing voices, and one voice saved her life. One night, she heard the message, "Move your bed." She heeded the message. Later, a truck drove through her bedroom wall, barely missing her.[44]

Allison did not use her intuitive gifts until she was an adult. She was working as an attorney in homicide when she discovered that by viewing homicide photos and touching the paperwork containing victims' names, she had visions of events that occurred before the person was killed.

Lisa Williams, a psychic medium, spiritual teacher, and best-selling author, played with a boy and girl spirit in her bedroom when she was a young child. From the corner of her bedroom, an elderly gentleman spirit watched her play with them. On one occasion, this gentleman followed Lisa as she joined her family for dinner. He screamed at her not to eat her peas, since she would die if she ate them. Frightened, she told her mother, but her mother could not see the man. Lisa was confused—she could see the man standing right beside her. She continued to tell her family about paranormal incidents she experienced, but they felt she had an "overactive imagination."[45] When she became an adult, Lisa embraced who she was. She became a world-renowned psychic medium, and continues to support others in learning about their spiritual gifts by teaching spiritual developmental courses around the world.

Another American psychic medium, Tamara Hermann, had a paranormal experience when she was nine years old. One day, while sitting at home with her sister and their family dog, Higgins, Tamara had a premonition. Sobbing, Tamara told her sister that Higgins was going to die. Her sister mocked her, called her silly, and told her she was acting like a nut. A few weeks later, Higgins was hit by a car and killed. A neighbor found Higgins' body beside the road. Tamara never spoke about her experience with her family again. Years later, other mystifying psychic and mediumship information came to her. So, she embraced her gifts.[46]

Many people who displayed intuitive abilities as children have several things in common: they did not feel safe or supported, they were overwhelmed, and they did not know what to do. Just imagine—what if these children had received the support they needed to develop their gifts and accept themselves as intuitives when they were younger?

---

[44] DuBois, Allison. *Don't Kiss Them Good-Bye*. Waterville, Me.: Thorndike Press, 2005. Kindle.
[45] Lisa Williams. "Intuitive Childhood," E-mail interview by author, August 11, 2021.
[46] Tamara Hermann, "Intuitive Childhood," E-mail interview by author, July 23, 2021.

Exercise: Research Professional Lightworkers

The goal for this exercise is to have intuitive children learn they are not alone when experiencing spiritual events; that there are adults who work in the spiritual business who had traumatic experiences as children while learning about spirits and energy.

Children should research professional lightworkers who have similar intuitive abilities. For example, if an intuitive child can communicate with people who have died, they should find a professional medium. If an intuitive child can see other people's auras, and know what others are thinking, they should find a professional psychic. If a child is into astrology, a professional astrologer would be a great research project. Once they get information about these professionals, these children need to decide, "What aspects of this person's life do I admire most? What skills do these lightworkers have? What goals should I develop so I can become a professional lightworker?"

Now What?

As a lightworker helping families with psychic children to manage their child's concerns and challenges, after doing a family's Intake session, you'll be developing and completing a customized plan to educate parents on how to help their intuitive child. Based on how the Family Plan unfolds, you'll need to determine when it is time for you to "graduate" the family from your spiritual support. It is always difficult to let your cherished clients go, but believe me, it will be harder on the family than on you. If a family is reluctant to be without your support and encouragement, you can place them on a consultation roster, checking in with them after a certain period to answer their questions about how they are doing at practicing the methods and techniques you have taught them, and guiding them over any "bumps in the road."

As your spiritual advisor relationship with each family ends, celebrate this milestone. You can mark the family's achievements in different ways—perhaps you'll provide a "Certificate of Spiritual Growth" to the family and child, give a unique gift to the child, or have a party. Be sure to acknowledge your contribution as well—congratulate yourself! Not only have you made a significant difference in a family's and a child's life; you've given them your love, time, energy, and knowledge. You've also provided tools so they can continue to awaken and take steps toward their spiritual wellness.

Spiritual wellness is vital in everyone's life. It helps people find purpose in their life's journey and makes a difference in their lives and in the world. I hope this has helped you and will inspire you to develop and expand your lightworker services to include helping psychic children and their families. The information in this book should guide you in developing a Family Service Plan with a variety of different holistic techniques. When you share your knowledge with families, they will feel empowered to help their child to fulfill his or her spiritual journey. You can make a big difference in these intuitive children's lives by working with one family at a time!

When you help children help embrace their intuitive gifts, your efforts will change their lives and will reap long-term rewards. When they are adults, they will know that because they were supported by their families and acquired knowledge to help them feel safe, they were able become inspiring lightworkers. They will feel that they too can help change the world, one day at a time. As His Holiness the 14th Dalai Lama stated: "Just as ripples spread out when a single pebble is dropped into water, the actions of individuals can have far-reaching effects."[47]

---

[47] https://strengthbasedliving.com/drop-a-pebble-create-a-positive-ripple/

9
Activity Pages

Day of week	Time of Day	Description of Activity	Duration

I am brave!

Design a protection shield.

Color the different chakras.

Color the outline of the auras with markers.

Draw a picture of your imaginary friend.

Draw a spirit that you have been seeing.

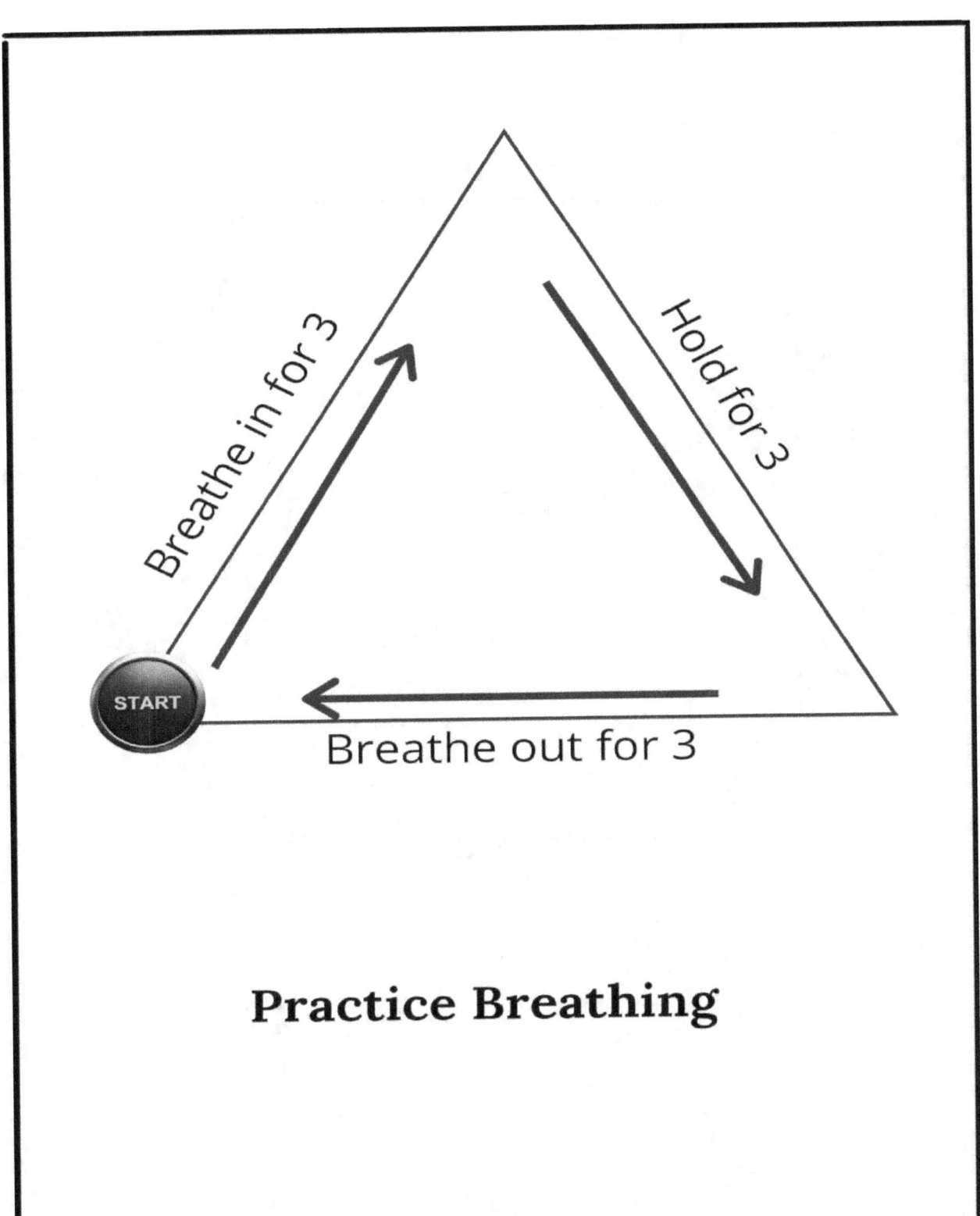

Practice Breathing

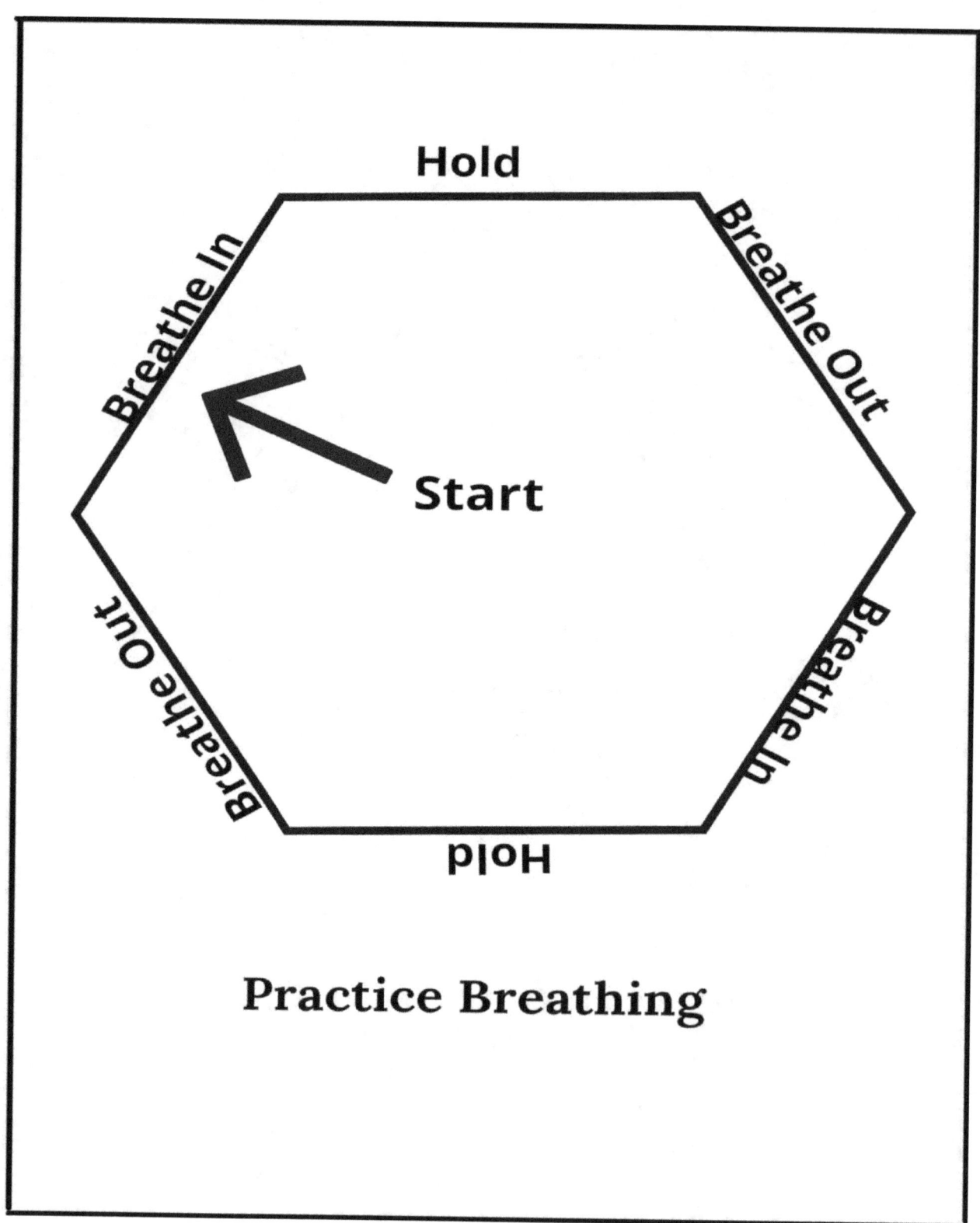

Practice Breathing

Write your favorite prayer.

 **Draw a picture of your dream.**

Draw the different emotions.

Happy

Sad

Excited

Mad

Surprised

Scared

What color goes with each emotion?

Happy

Sad

Excited

Mad

Surprised

Scared

Draw things that you make you happy.

Draw things that you make you excited.

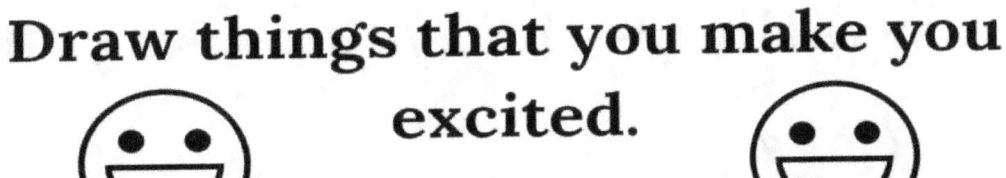

Draw things that you make you mad.

Draw things that you make you surprised.

Draw things that you make you scared.

I'm unique!

Glossary

Clair:
A prefix meaning "clear" in French. Clair senses are different types of psychic sensitivities which give us information about an event, person, object, or location.

Dark Entity:
A powerful evil force that attaches to a person, object, or location. They derive energy from living entities and may interfere with their emotions in a negative manner.

Ethereal Realm:
Also known as the astral plane. Our souls travel through the ethereal plane in our astral body before we are born, and when we die, our consciousness resides in this realm. The Ethereal Realm is a part of the Divine and other spiritual beings.

Lightworker:
Someone who has been incarnated for the main purpose of making the world a better place by healing, helping, and uplifting others. This individual might be considered an empath, intuitive, psychic, medium, energy worker, messenger, or a light warrior.

Pineal Gland:
Located in the middle of the brain, the pineal gland secretes the hormone melatonin, and is known to activate and give energy to the third-eye chakra. When calcium deposits grow on the pineal gland, they can affect the production of melatonin and cause hormonal imbalances, sleep disturbances, and thyroid problems. Some metaphysicians feel that calcification can also block the energy the third-eye chakra needs in order to activate.

Reader:
In the context of this book, "reader" is defined as the person who is completing a psychic or mediumship reading.

Sitter:
A "sitter" is the client paying for and receiving a reading from a professional lightworker. The spiritual service rendered may be a psychic or a mediumship reading, healing session, or other holistic service.

Spirit Communicator:
A spiritual entity—such as a loved one who has died, a spirit guide, or an angel—who communicates with people who are living.

Spiritual World:

People who practice Spiritualism believe the spiritual world is a realm where spirit (the Divine, angels, ascended masters, elders, master guides, loved ones in spirit, etc.) dwell.

References

Books:

DuBois, Allison. *Don't Kiss Them Good-Bye*. Waterville, Me.: Thorndike Press, 2005. Kindle.

Kramarik, Akiane. *Akiane: Her Life, Her Art, Her Poetry*. Nashville: Thomas Nelson, 2017. Print.

Miller, Lisa. *The Spiritual Child: The New Science on Parenting for Health and Lifelong Thriving*. New York: Picador/St. Martin's Press, 2016. Kindle.

Orloff, Judith. *The Empath's Survival Guide: Life Strategies for Sensitive People*. Boulder, CO: Sounds True, Inc., 2018.

Stillman, William. *Autism and the God Connection: Redefining the Autistic Experience through Extraordinary Accounts of Spiritual Giftedness*. Naperville, IL: Sourcebooks, Inc., 2006. Kindle.

Virtue, Doreen. *The Care and Feeding of Indigo Children*. Alexandra, N.S.W.: Hay House, 2006. Kindle.

Wiseman, Sara. *Your Psychic Child: How to Raise Intuitive and Spiritually Gifted Kids of All Ages*. St. Paul, MN: Llewellyn, 2011. Kindle.

Web Resources:

"Autism Statistics and Facts." Autism Speaks. Accessed September 26, 2021. https://www.autismspeaks.org/autism-statistics-asd.

Blom.10, "Are You an Indigo Child Too?" The Psychology of Extraordinary Beliefs, April 16, 2019. https://u.osu.edu/vanzandt/2019/04/16/indigo-child-movement/.

Cramer, Charles, and Kim Grant. "Surrealist Techniques: Automatism" (Article). Khan Academy. Accessed September 26,2021. https://www.khanacademy.org/humanities/art-1010/dada-and-surrealism/xdc974a79: surrealism/a/surrealist-techniques-automatism.

Delgran, Lois. "What Is Spirituality?" Taking Charge of Your Health & Wellbeing. Accessed September 26, 2021. https://www.takingcharge.csh.umn.edu/what-spirituality.

Guc, Ahmet. "Satanism and Youth's Quest for Identity." *The Fountain*. Accessed September 26, 2021. https://fountainmagazine.com/2004/issue-45-january-march-2004/satanism-and-youths-quest-for-identity.

Harrison, Laura A., Anaastansiya Kats, Marian E. Williams, and Lisa Aziz-Zadeh. "The Importance of Sensory Processing in Mental Health: A Proposed Addition to the Research Domain Criteria (Rdoc) and Suggestions for Rdoc 2.0." *Frontiers in Psychology 10* (2019). https://pubmed.ncbi.nlm.nih.gov/30804830/.

Hart, T., and Erin E. Zellars. "[Pdf] When Imaginary Companions Are Sources of Wisdom: Semantic Scholar." [PDF] January 1, 1970. https://www.semanticscholar.org/paper/When-Imaginary-Companions-Are-Sources-of-Wisdom-Hart-Zellars/2107369fa6d900bce4b34bc4bb71acdbc1c9dd0a.

History.com Staff. "Did Abraham Lincoln Predict His Own Death?" History.com. A&E Television Network, October 31, 2012. https://www.history.com/news/did-abraham-lincoln-predict-his-own-death.

Larson , Cynthia Sue. "Many Children See Auras." RealityShifters. Accessed September 26, 2021. http://realityshifters.com/pages/articles/childrenseeauras.html.

Lee, Sandra L. "Satanism-Some Behaviors May Be a Warning." *The Lewiston Tribune*, June 7, 1992. Assessed on September 15, 2021 https://lmtribune.com/northwest/satanism-some-behaviors-may-be-a-warning/article_416eb070-a314-5866-9be9-3a1976fd5638.html.

Malavika, and Malavika. "Chakras: 7 Year Development Life-Cycles." Malavika, January 11, 2014. https://hellomalavika.com/2012/09/22/chakras-7-year-development-life-cycles/.

Mandalis, Liane. "Clairsentience." Unimed Living. Accessed September 26, 2021.. https://www.unimedliving.com/unimedpedia/word-index/unimedpedia-clairsentience.html.

Monroe, Alissa. "Beginner's Guide to Clairalience – the Psychic Gift of Smelling Spirits." *Psychics 4 Today*. Accessed September 26, 2021. https://www.psychics4today.com/paranormal-smells/.

Nielsen, Becca. "Different Modes of Sensing - Part 6: Clairgustance." Core Potentials, October 29, 2020. https://www.corepotentials.ca/blog/different-modes-sensing-clairgustance.

Powers, Albert R., Megan S. Kelley, and Philip R. Corlett. "Varieties of Voice-Hearing: Psychics and the Psychosis Continuum." *Schizophrenia Bulletin* 43, no. 1 (2016): 84–98. https://doi.org/10.1093/schbul/sbw133.

Rose, Nicole. "Psychic Dreams: What You Need to Know About This ESP Phenomenon." Medium. Dream Codes, August 28, 2020. https://medium.com/dream-codes/psychic-dreams-how-to-know-if-youve-had-one-f0839c5d29eb.

Rudy, Lisa Jo. "Autism and Spirituality." Verywell Health. Accessed April 18, 2021. https://www.verywellhealth.com/autism-and-spirituality-260300.

Saunders, David T, Helen Clegg, Graham Smith, and Chris A Roe. "Lucid dreaming incidence: a quality effects meta-analysis of 50 years of research." *Consciousness and Cognition.* U.S. National Library of Medicine. Accessed September 27, 2021. https://pubmed.ncbi.nlm.nih.gov/27337287/.

Shardlow, Giselle. "5 Breathing Exercises for Kids for Calm and Focus." Kids Yoga Stories. Yoga and mindfulness resources for kids, January 18, 2021. https://www.kidsyogastories.com/breathing-exercises-for-kids/.

--. "Chakras for Kids: Learn about their Emotions through Yoga Poses for Kids." Kids Yoga Stories. Yoga and mindfulness resources for kids, April 20, 2020. https://www.kidsyogastories.com/chakras-for-kids/.

Spencer, Maya. "What Is Spirituality? A Personal Exploration." Royal College of Psychiatrists, 2012. https://www.rcpsych.ac.uk/docs/default-source/members/sigs/spirituality-spsig/what-is-spirituality-maya-spencer-x.pdf?sfvrsn=f28df052_2.

St. Maarten, Anthon "Claircognizance - the Gift of Psychic Knowing." LinkedIn, February 6, 2021. https://www.linkedin.com/pulse/claircognizance-gift-psychic-knowing-anthon-st-maarten.

Stelter, Gretchen. "Chakras: A Beginner's Guide to the 7 Chakras." Healthline Media, December 19, 2016. https://www.healthline.com/health/fitness-exercise/7-chakras#Chakra-101.

Stokes, Victoria. "Intuitive Empaths: Signs, Types, Downsides, and Self-Care." Healthline Media, April 6, 2021. https://www.healthline.com/health/intuitive-empaths.

Tanaaz. "The 7 Layers of Your Aura." Forever Conscious, October 10, 2020. https://foreverconscious.com/7-layers-aura.

Typically Tropical. "The 11 Most Powerful Types of Spirit Guides on Your Team." Typically Topical, September 4, 2021. https://typicallytopical.com/types-of-spirit-guides/.

Tillmans, Maria daVenza. "Children, Intuitive Knowledge & Philosophy." *Philosophy Now: a magazine of ideas.* Accessed September 26, 2021. https://philosophynow.org/issues/119/Children_Intuitive_Knowledge_and_Philosophy.

Wenig, Marsha. "Why Kids Need Yoga as Much as We Do." Yoga Journal, September 2, 2021. https://www.yogajournal.com/teach/teaching-methods/yoga-for-kids/.

"What Is Clairvoyance?" Clairvoyant Center of Hawaii, October 29, 2020. https://clairvoyanthawaii.com/what-is-clairvoyance/.

Wojciechowski, Debbie. "What Is a Medium?" Debbie Wojciechowski — Evidential Medium, November 11, 2019. https://mediumdebbie.com/blog/2019/10/30/what-is-a-medium.

URLs:

https://www.brainyquote.com/quotes/marie_curie_389010 "Medium." IMDb.com, January 3, 2005. https://www.imdb.com/title/tt0412175/.

https://www.nurturedneurons.com/quotes-about-play/. 50 of the Greatest and Most Inspirational Quotes About Play.

https://www.perinormal.org.

https://psychicryanmichaels.com.

https://strengthbasedliving.com/drop-a-pebble-create-a-positive-ripple/

Interviews:

Hermann, Tamara. "Intuitive Childhood." E-mail interview by author. July 23, 2021.

Williams, Lisa. "Intuitive Childhood." E-mail interview by author. August 11, 2021.

About the Author

Michelle Henderson, M. Ed. worked in education as a teacher, educational diagnostician, and behavior analyst for thirty years. While teaching children with autism, she wrote a book titled *A Three Element Social Skill Program: Instruction, Drama, and Technology*. In 2006, she opened IASIS Learning Center, a non-profit organization teaching children social skills through drama techniques. After retiring from education, knowing she was going to serve the Divine and offer spiritual services, Michelle obtained her Ordained Ministry from the Universal Life Church Ministries in 2019. In 2021, Michelle became a Certified Spiritual Advisor, earning Psychic and Medium Certificates through the Lisa Williams International School of Spiritual Development. With the knowledge she has obtained through her lifelong work with children, she is passionate about helping intuitive children embrace their gifts. Michelle also shares her innovative ideas with other lightworkers, giving them direction about supporting families of intuitive children.

To connect with Michelle and to access continued strategies on *Spiritual Nurturing for Intuitive Children*, visit MichelleHendersonMedium.com and get even more resources, exercises, and helpful content to support your journey.

www.ingramcontent.com/pod-product-compliance
Lightning Source LLC
Chambersburg PA
CBHW080845120626
46553CB00009B/2572